THE
PINNACLE
OF
PRESENCE

First published in June 2020 by Sheila Wherry
www.eiexecutive.com.au.
Copyright © 2020, Sheila Wherry

The moral rights of the author have been asserted.
All rights reserved. Except as permitted under the Australian Copyright Act 1968 (for example, a fair dealing for the purposes of study, research, criticism or review), no part of this book may be reproduced, stored in a retrieval system, communicated or transmitted in any form or by any means without prior written permission. All inquiries should be made to the publisher at sheila.wherry@eiexecutive.com.au
Extracts from The Fearless Organization by Amy Edmondson (2019) and Reading the Room: Group Dynamics for Coaches and Leaders (2012) reproduced with permission by John Wiley and Sons Inc. All other extracts reproduced with permission from authors.

Disclaimer
The material in this publication is of the nature of general comment only and does not represent professional advice. It is not intended to provide specific guidance for any particular circumstances and it should not be relied upon for any decision to take action or not to take action on any matter which it covers. Reader should obtain professional advice where appropriate before making any such decision. To the maximum extent permitted by law, the author and publisher disclaim all responsibility and liability to any person, arising directly or indirectly from any person taking or not taking action based on the information in this book.

This book uses a composite of client stories to highlight key points. Names & details have been anonymised to protect individual privacy.

Edited by Lu Sexton
Cover design by Liz Seymour
Page design by Lorna Hendry
Printed by Ingram Spark

ISBN: (paperback) 978-0-6488729-0-0
ISBN: (ebook) 978-0-6488729-1-7

THE PINNACLE OF PRESENCE

How great leaders connect, instil trust & get the right results

Sheila Wherry

TESTIMONIALS

Sheila's genuine passion for her chosen field is almost infectious. She is thought-provoking and insightful – coaching and challenging as required.

Through warmth, humour, perception and expertise, Sheila encouraged me to view work situations through multiple lenses and helped me build tools to respond. She remains a silent supportive voice urging me forward. I value the insights Sheila helped me develop on various occasions over the years, and highly recommend her as a professional advocate and coach for individuals and teams alike.

Aideen O'Donovan, Head of Finance and Decision Support

Sheila is a consummate professional and highly regarded coach. She has consistently received outstanding feedback and results for clients, and is strongly committed to her own continuous professional development. I would have no hesitation in recommending Sheila's coaching services.

Dr Crissa Sumner, Head of Employee Experience Solution Strategy

Sheila is an empathetic and highly skilled coach, who will help you to unlock and realise your full potential; on both a professional and personal level. Through working with Sheila as my executive coach, I have been able to fine tune my self- awareness and reconnect with my creativity as a professional, and an artist. I am now painting fearlessly again.
Beverley Farrell, Category Manager, IT Strategic Sourcing

Sheila's guidance, although sometimes confronting, was always incredibly insightful. She is an inspirational coach who lives what she teaches, and I still reflect on many of the lessons she provided me.
Julie Bown, General Manager Mission Solutions

In the time that Sheila managed our coach team, she showed herself to be a highly capable leadership and executive coach and commercially-minded manager, with a unique ability to collaborate across multi-functional teams and build connections with colleagues and client alike. She is well known within our team for her empathetic, supportive, and performance-minded approach. Sheila also consistently received strong feedback from her coaching clients, and demonstrated a clear and unwavering passion for high quality coaching and client focus.
Lorraine Smith, (Associate) Director, Talent Management NSW and ACT

I have had the great privilege of being coached by Sheila for over 12 months. At the beginning, it was confronting, but now I am so grateful, Sheila has helped me grow professionally and personally. I feel I am a better leader and a more resilient and happier person as a result. Highly recommended!
Julie Collins, Head of Compliance

Sheila is an inspiring and innovative coach in both individual and team situations. Her innate ability to quickly recognise and work with a team dynamic holds her in good stead, to bring out the best in each participant in a team workshop environment. This results in high performing individuals moving into a space of psychological safety, where they can work together to become a high performing team.

My personal experience and the feedback from my team regarding Sheila's workshops and coaching, has been tremendous. I have witnessed improvements in resilience and optimism. In addition to increased ability to strategise and problem solve in a fast-paced environment.
Amalie Smith, Head of Network Delivery

This book is dedicated to my tribe:

My family, we've come so far, and I'm so thankful for your love, individually and as a family.

*My close friends. My life is richer with you in it.
Kylie, my partner in life and my haven.*

And Connor, my greatest gift and a presence maestro. I'm so proud of all that you are.

Contents

Introduction	3
PART 1: NAVIGATING THE CHALLENGES OF MODERN LEADERSHIP	7
CHAPTER 1 Relationships to results	9
CHAPTER 2 Trust. Connect. Collaborate.	17
PART 2: THE PINNACLE OF PRESENCE	29
CHAPTER 3 Connecting with self	31
CHAPTER 4 Inner Presence	51
CHAPTER 5 Leadership Presence	81
CHAPTER 6 Team Presence	123
Over to you	151
Related reading	154
Ways to keep in touch and work together	158
Author bio	159

INTRODUCTION

Imagine working with a team that was open, curious and safe enough to talk and think through problems together, to find innovative solutions, without the risk of negative consequences or interpersonal fear.

Imagine feeling like you no longer have to keep working harder and pedalling faster to succeed in this complex, fast-paced, hyper-connected world – and that you no longer have to come up with all the solutions yourself.

Imagine starting each work day feeling grounded and invigorated, confident in how you are leading yourself and others, clear you are making the right choices. Life may be hectic, but you feel a sense of ease and calm. You have a clear direction. You are present.

Fantasy or possibility?

If you read this book and put in some reflective work, it's a definite possibility.

For many years I have had the privilege of supporting smart, brave and dedicated leaders to improve their ability to work effectively with others to produce results.

They have moved from being stuck or overwhelmed, to being empowered to release their own potential, and the potential of their teams. Witnessing these transformations has galvanised me to put down the steps that I have seen work again and again.

There is no cookie cutter solution of course, and no two leaders are the same. The approach I offer is a framework, and it starts with trust and connection.

The central piece of work these leaders do is to build their capacity to connect – with themselves and with others. This is an essential starting point because:

- connection is the key to cultivating relationships

- relationships are the key to collaboration

- collaboration is fundamental if you want successful results.

You can't bypass relationships to get to results. Not in the long term. Not sustainably.

Simple? Yes. Easy? No. Or at least it takes some practice. And it takes a process.

My process is The Pinnacle of Presence framework and incorporates three distinct domains — Inner Presence, Leadership Presence and Team Presence.

You may have heard and read about presence. It's a nebulous term that means different things to different people. The main thing that people agree on is that leaders need *it*, (whatever *it* is).

Let's simplify it for a moment and say that presence is bringing your best self to the role of leadership. To bring your best self to the role of leadership you need to understand yourself – your inner drivers, your behaviours, your strengths and weaknesses – and you need to understand the effect these have on others. This is why I have expanded the concept of presence to the three domains:

- **Inner Presence** – Being self-empowered to fully accept and believe in yourself, confident to show others the real you.

- **Leadership Presence** – Projecting your Inner Presence outwards, signalling that you have what it takes to lead others.

- **Team Presence** – Cultivating an environment that empowers teams to collaborate, learn and innovate.

Or to put it more simply:

- Inner Presence – why you do it
- Leadership Presence – how you do it
- Team Presence – doing it together

The presence you bring to yourself and your teams can be the greatest gift to yourself and those you lead. If you are feeling overwhelmed by the relentless demands of your work, presence will help you feel calm and confident. If you are feeling frustrated by your working relationships or by missing out on promotion opportunities, it will help you generate connection and credibility. If your teams are fragmented and underperforming, it will help you cultivate collaboration and creativity.

This book shows you how.

I will show you practical ways to set aside the individual, leadership and team habits and behaviours that aren't working for you. In their place, I've provided a roadmap to a new way of living and leading – more thoughtfully, more intentionally – using human connection as the key.

I will take you through a process to support your own self-reflection and learning. We will work together, as I do with my clients, to discover your inner resources and find new ways to manage the challenges of modern leadership.

PART 1

NAVIGATING THE CHALLENGES OF MODERN LEADERSHIP

Increasingly, the sources of competitive advantage will come from the capacity to build cooperative partnerships across various ecosystems. That will bring to the centre stage the capacity to create cultures of cooperation, trust and inclusion.

LYNDA GRATTON,
PROFESSOR OF MANAGEMENT PRACTICE,
LONDON BUSINESS SCHOOL

CHAPTER 1

RELATIONSHIPS TO RESULTS

The door opens and my new client walks in. Let's call her 'Ash'. Ash's face is taut. Her brow is drawn together and her forehead furrowed. Unconsciously, as we start to chat, she clenches her hands tightly together. With a few gentle questions, her words start to flow, then gain momentum. Ash explains that she is overwhelmed. Frustrated. Drained. Her problems are multiplying, and she doesn't know how to manage them. She can't understand it. She's a professional and, until recently, confident in her abilities. Now she's not so sure. She just can't see a path forward.

Nearly every leader I work with, no matter what challenges or opportunities they face, has a common story. They have worked hard to get to where they are, and now they have hit a snag and are struggling to produce their best results.

It could be that they:

- have lost their zest for leading

- are missing out on promotion opportunities

- feel overwhelmed, or burnt out, or are on the cusp of burnout

- are frustrated by those around them – their manager, their peers, their stakeholders – and the relationship has frayed

- feel confused about whether the choices they are making are the right ones

- are receiving feedback that their behaviour is being portrayed in a negative light

- feel their team are disengaged or demotivated.

They know they have reached a stumbling block but they don't know what's causing it or how to untangle themselves from it.

Add to this that they are expected to be on and available 24/7 in this fast-paced, hyper-connected world of work, and they feel they have to pedal harder, faster and longer to keep ahead of the curve. This can leave them

CHAPTER 1: RELATIONSHIPS TO RESULTS

feeling overwhelmed and frustrated, unclear about what to prioritise to turn their ship around, and how to navigate the waters ahead. Does this sound familiar?

There's a central theme to these problems: their management strategies are no longer working. They are more focussed on results than relationships, which is a leadership style that is no longer effective in the complex times in which we are living and working. Why not? Because relationships are the building blocks of effective teams, and in today's complex world working in teams is no longer optional, it's imperative. The problems we are facing are so complex that teamwork and collective thinking are essential to providing innovative solutions, creative problem solving and getting work done.

This is an argument supported by global accounting firm Ernst & Young in their 2013 report entitled 'The Power of Many'. In this report, they showed the results of a survey of 821 senior executives. An overwhelming majority believed that the ability to develop and manage teams was essential for future competitiveness. These executives felt they spent over 50% of their time on team activities. This really brings the ability of leaders to effectively manage and work with their teams into sharp focus. The report states that, 'Leadership in a team setting is much less about command and control, and more about getting the most out of a diverse and experienced group of individuals.'

Until recently, leaders used rational cause-and-effect

strategies to come up with solutions. Certainty and predictability meant you could use your expertise, rational mind and a more commanding or hierarchical style of leadership. In fact, you were paid to use your expertise and come up with the answers.

But that certainty and predictability is no longer there. Our world of work has shifted unrecognisably and will continue to do so. We no longer work nine to five, remain with one company for decades, or switch off like we used to when leaving the office. We don't sit at our desk in one location, and many of us don't sit together with our teams each day. Virtual meetings have replaced face-to-face meetings and teams have become more geographically dispersed and diverse. Changes will continue. They are hurtling towards us at speed and we can't plan for what's next. We don't know what 'next' is.

In this new world of work, leaders today are like racing car drivers, but they are on a new and different racetrack.

In the past, drivers pulled into the pits when their tyres needed changing. The pit stop team practiced and, through their coordinated effort, could change all four tyres in under two seconds! Astonishing. The driver then raced back out onto the course. It was a level playing field; all drivers needed to make these pit stops. But the driver with the competitive edge was the one with the team who worked well together and honed their art.

Not anymore.

CHAPTER 1: RELATIONSHIPS TO RESULTS

The 'racing-car driving' leaders of today need more than speed and consistency from their teams if they want their business to maintain a competitive edge.

As a leader, you used to drive around the racetrack before the event to plan, prepare and visualise tactics. Now the track ahead is shifting and reshaping before your very eyes. You can't see what is around the next bend. Your tyre requirements keep changing based on the unpredictable new track. Your team must calculate what tyres you need at any given moment. More pit stops, less time, and harder choices.

As the driver, what do you do in this situation? Be clear on your purpose: to win the race. Absolutely. Be clear on operational aspects, such as making sure your team is highly skilled and motivated. Of course.

Yet so much remains unknown.

To remain agile and thrive, you must shift your thinking and ask: what does this team and our stakeholders need? And your team and all other stakeholders must do the same.

As a client recently shared, 'My senior leadership team, and the wider team generally, talk of change fatigue. I get it. But it isn't going to change. Our business, as it currently stands, won't exist in five years. Our purpose will be the same but how we achieve success will be totally unrecognisable from any strategy we are employing now'.

You can no longer be expected to have all the answers.

Now more than ever you need the brains trust of your whole team.

Thinking about this racing car scenario, the key for your team to maintain competitive advantage and produce effective outcomes is their ability to rapidly, effectively and intentionally **talk and think together, with agility**. It is essential that the leader and their crew are openly discussing issues, making suggestions, owning mistakes, coming up with potential solutions together: tweaking and nudging, and all this must be done at speed. It takes a team that feels safe enough to do this together. One that understands the necessity of speaking up, giving feedback, and challenging ideas and each other. Respectfully. One that can do this within their team, but also across teams: a network of teams talking and thinking together.

Leaders today are not necessarily driving the car either. Their role may be best served in the pits, creating the right environment for their team to keep navigating the changing path ahead.

As a client shared, 'I work hard to empower my senior leaders. I say: You are my leadership team. The best experience for me is if you can come to a common view before coming to me. I don't want to be the conduit for decision making. Make decisions. I will always back you, as long as you aren't shooting from the hip. You can't turn the car if you aren't moving'.

This leader is explicitly encouraging her team to

CHAPTER 1: RELATIONSHIPS TO RESULTS

question, challenge, have hard conversations and keep driving forward. Collectively. Interdependently.

Yet it doesn't stop there. There is a need for end-to-end accountability across the business, and an avoidance of siloed thinking. There's a need to draw out connections *between* teams, as well as within teams.

My client demonstrates this as she explains, 'I work exceptionally hard to build trust with *all* my stakeholders. I seek to connect in order to understand their needs'.

My client understands the fundamental need to focus on cultivating **relationships** to get to the **results**.

And to do this she starts with trust.

CHAPTER 2

TRUST. CONNECT. COLLABORATE.

It turns out that trust is in fact earned in the smallest of moments. It is earned not through heroic deeds, or even highly visible actions, but through paying attention, listening, and gestures of genuine care and connection.

BRENÉ BROWN
DARE TO LEAD

The traditional idea of leaders as strong and forceful people who lack warmth is outdated. We now know that great leaders start by gaining trust, listening, and developing empathy and emotional intelligence. Whether you're talking about leadership, friendship, parenting or any human relationship, people need to know that you care, that you have good intentions and that they can trust you. Without this vital element they will not get behind you or the relationship.

People only value a leader when they trust them – abilities come second, argues Amy Cuddy, a social psychologist, author and speaker. She also underlines the value of being a good listener as it is an excellent way to gain trust. I agree.

Great leaders know how to balance warmth and strength. And they invariably lead with warmth.

At the outbreak of the COVID-19 pandemic, New Zealand's Prime Minister Jacinda Ardern found a perfect balance of strength and warmth.

She held a press conference on 23 March 2020 in which she announced the decision to act quickly and firmly in an attempt to get ahead of the pandemic. She outlined unprecedented measures, aware of the huge instability and disruption they would cause. She asked the nation to get behind her. She acknowledged that it was going to be difficult but was firm in her convictions. She did not waiver. She was clear, unapologetic and strong. At the same time, she showed she cared. She finished her speech asking the New Zealand people to, 'Be kind and strong'. She offered strength and warmth, and she asked for the same in return.

Nearly two months later she polled as New Zealand's most popular prime minister in a century.

Leaders who choose to focus on strength and credentials, and less on trust and warmth, risk triggering fear and dysfunctional behaviours in the workplace.

This is the point made by Amy Cuddy, Matthew

CHAPTER 2: TRUST. CONNECT. COLLABORATE

Kohut and John Neffinger in the *Harvard Business Review* article 'Connect Then Lead'. These authors explain the need to avoid fear because it limits the cognitive potential of your people, their creativity and their ability to problem solve, all key qualities needed in our knowledge economy. Fear is also a major cause of employee disengagement.

A 2018 study cited in the *Harvard Business Review* article, 'Does Your Leadership Style Scare Your Employees?', explains that managing employees with pressure tactics results in more than a 90% increase in the predicted turnover of employees. Using more inspirational tactics translated roughly to a 68% decrease in likely turnover.

Let's face it, we all know when our manager isn't in a great mood, and these feelings can spread across the team. This is called emotional contagion.

Joshua Freedman is the CEO of Six Seconds, an author and an expert in emotional intelligence. His book *At The Heart of Leadership* explores how emotional contagion flows from the group leader to their team. He cites a study published in the *Journal of Organisational and Leadership Design*, entitled 'Quitting the Boss? The Role of Manager Influence Tactics and Employee Emotional Engagement in Voluntary Turnover' which found, 'the positive mood of the leader positively influenced group members at both the individual and collective level, with the opposite happening for a leader's negative mood. The leader's positive mood also had a subsequent influence on group coordination and effort'. This study concludes that, 'managers who inspire rather than pressure their employees are better able to retain talent, in part, because they create an emotional connection between their employees and their work'.

Some of my clients have embarked on a coaching program with me because their people have started to disengage or, worse still, they are creating fear and anger in the people they work with and/or lead. Others have become so focused on results and short-term outcomes that they've lost awareness of the impact they're having on those around them. They are on autopilot, responding to the rapid nature of their workload and overwhelming demands.

Let's return to Ash from Chapter 1.

> Ash is a senior leader in a global corporation. She has a team of 235, with five direct reports. As we start our initial coaching session, Ash appears a little more relaxed than the previous time we met. When I enquire about this, she explains the relief she feels at having a coach – someone to partner with, to work through her challenges and find a way forward. We start by exploring her context: the role itself, what she enjoys about it, her strengths and areas she's looking to develop. She smiles as she shares. She is technically strong,

CHAPTER 2: TRUST. CONNECT. COLLABORATE

and she builds rapport easily with others. She has created a solid team and they know she cares about them. She pauses, sighs and continues. In recent times, however, she has received feedback from her direct manager that she is upsetting stakeholders in the business. It has also been noticed that she is allowing her frustration to show in the team. She stops. Unsure on where to go from here.

Ash is smart. She's navigated her way into a senior leadership position. She's dedicated. She's driven. She has a family and a close circle of friends. By all accounts she is succeeding in life. Yet something isn't working and she needs to find a solution for herself, fast. Her actions and behaviours are getting noticed by those around her: the senior leadership team, her stakeholders, peers and direct reports.

I reassure her. We will work together to map out a path back to clarity, confidence and ease. She takes a breath and smiles.

As part of Ash's coaching program, I gather feedback from a selection of direct reports, peers, senior leaders and her manager. Key themes emerge. Everyone respects Ash. They all value her

> input and want her to continue to speak up with expertise. Yet they have noticed that in recent times she has become more direct, blunt and frustrated. Her stakeholders are starting to resent the way she pushes her solutions onto them, rather than asking for their input and getting their buy-in. Her team have watched as she rolls her eyes when referring to other stakeholders, and they are starting to take on her negative feelings. This is impacting team performance and engagement. Some peers are reluctant to approach her.

Ash's story is a common one. Leaders I work with are often highly educated, technically strong, and have successfully climbed the corporate ladder, yet they need to find new ways to lead. In Ash's case, as in many cases, the reality is that relationships have eroded, or have not been developed well in the first place.

Ash had lost focus on the need to connect – both with herself and with others. She was no longer present.

What steps did Ash take to return to success and fulfilment? She started by accepting that she needed to understand how and why her behaviour was contributing to the problem. To do this she carved out space to build a self-reflective habit. She took the time to understand her emotions and patterns of behaviour: why she reacted as opposed to consciously respond in high stake situations. And the more she reflected, the more

CHAPTER 2: TRUST. CONNECT. COLLABORATE

she understood herself and was able to self-regulate. She connected to self.

She came to understand that this wasn't a tick box solution, this was an ongoing self-reflective practice. Yet the more she developed her emotional literacy, the more grounded she became. She had jumped off the emotional rollercoaster; she had the tools to self-manage.

She found a place of calm even in high stake situations.

From here, she looked inwards and realised she had choices. And by doing the work of Inner Presence, she learnt to make them. She developed a strong sense of self, got clear on what gave her life meaning, and she created a vision of what she aspires to be. She felt grounded, and her inner confidence and self-worth flourished.

This is the first domain, Inner Presence, which I define as: Being self-empowered to fully accept and believe in yourself, confident to show others the real you.

Ash built on this foundational level of presence and started to look outwards. She reflected on how she was behaving with others and the impact this was having on those around her. To produce results, she realised, not only did she need to bring her best self to the role, she needed to adopt leadership behaviours that built trust and connection, as well as demonstrate strength and warmth.

This is the second domain, Leadership Presence: Projecting your Inner Presence outwards, signalling that you have what it takes to lead others.

Finally, she turned her attention to how to produce results with others. How to navigate team dynamics, adopt intentional communication and learn to foster a team environment that generates collective problem solving, innovative solutions and ongoing learning – not only within Ash's team, but across teams. A team of teams.

This is the final domain, Team Presence: Creating an environment that empowers teams to collaborate, learn and innovate.

By walking through the three domains of presence, Ash had greater insight into what she needed to bring to any conversation or context to keep it moving forward productively. She cultivated the capacity to generate respectful and robust relationships – relationships that produced results.

> Ash walked confidently into our final session. She smiled broadly; her face was relaxed. She said she felt she was doing a good job and she recognised the hard work she had put in to develop her newfound sense of confidence and ease. This had taken conscious practice. She realised she had always had the answers and the capability, it was really about carving out time to pause and reflect, and to have the support and structure to ensure she kept her aspirations front of mind.

CHAPTER 2: TRUST. CONNECT. COLLABORATE

She shared her delight at having a stronger sense of self, while knowing how to adapt as necessary to lead others and to be perceived in the way she intended. The pace remains relentless, she shared, but she was more relaxed, knowing she had the tools to navigate her way forward, and she was doing this alongside others. She had also come to see this was a dynamic process. She couldn't tick the boxes and say she had worked on her 'presence'. It was a constantly evolving practice.

We finished her sessions by reflecting on what she remains challenged by, and what the next steps were for her. She said there was still work to be done in fostering a team dynamic that promoted ongoing high performance and engagement, but she and the team were making progress, and they were committed to this. They were all familiar with the concept of psychological safety. They had talked about key behaviours that were accepted by the team, to drive such an environment (for instance active listening and giving feedback in the moment), as well as those that weren't (such as gossiping and blaming others); together they decided what they would tolerate and what they would call out. They had a language and framework, and Ash was working

> hard to respond positively when others demonstrated these behaviours; aware that it was important to be a role model for such behaviour.

These domains – Inner Presence, Leadership Presence and Team Presence – are not distinct concepts. While I have separated them out to give you a simple and accessible framework to follow, they are interrelated. I provide you with this framework as scaffolding to support your thinking and reflection.

Please bear in mind that this is a framework, not a prescription. I don't know your particular circumstances, so I don't pretend to have all the answers for you. What I can do is support you by offering signposts and suggestions for new approaches, as I do with my clients.

No two clients are the same. We all approach our challenges differently with unique ways of seeing the world. As an executive coach, I need to be agile and attentive to my clients' needs. It would not be productive if I simply rolled out a framework and went through it in a linear fashion. I follow many theories and models – but I hold them lightly. I refer to them as needed. They hold me to account, ensuring I am following a structure; they are part of my toolkit. At the same time, it is important that I work with what emerges in each session, and that I respond to what my client needs. I call this macro and micro tracking. Tracking the big picture of where my client wants to get to, while at the same time

CHAPTER 2: TRUST. CONNECT. COLLABORATE

noticing the subtle nuances along the way, addressing what emerges and what needs attending to.

I ask you to do the same as you work through this book. It is a guide, it is not 'the' answer.

I'm a trekker and each year I do a multi-day trek with my son. When we set off into nature we take a map. This helps us move from point to point, but it does not provide the answers to all situations we may face along the way. If we wander off course, the map offers a reference point and a visual guide to support us as we think and discuss the best route forward.

So, with that, I ask you to pick up the map – The Pinnacle of Presence – and let's trek together.

PART 2

THE PINNACLE OF PRESENCE

CHAPTER 3

CONNECTING WITH SELF

*We shall not cease from exploration,
and the end of all our exploring will be to
arrive where we started and know the place
for the first time.*

TS ELIOT

To develop the capacity to connect with others, we must start by understanding and connecting with ourselves.

Being connected with self means becoming aware of our internal thoughts, feelings, behaviours and embodied sensations. This invites improved relationships with ourselves and with others, as well as our ability to perform.

Connecting with self begins with recognising what you are feeling and understanding why you are feeling it. This is emotional self-awareness. Understanding the what and why behind your feelings gives you the power to *respond* to situations, as opposed to *react*. This is emotional regulation.

These go hand in hand: the more aware you are of your emotions the greater your ability to regulate them.

Emotional self-awareness and regulation are part of a larger framework called emotional intelligence, or EQ. Psychologists and authors Peter Salovey and John Mayer coined the term emotional intelligence in the 1990s, in their groundbreaking article *Emotional Intelligence* published in Imagination, Cognition and Personality Journal. They defined it as 'the ability to perceive emotions, to access and generate emotions so as to assist thought, to understand emotions and emotional knowledge, and to reflectively regulate emotions so as to promote emotional and intellectual growth'.

Emotional self-awareness

Emotions are data: they can be used to inform your decision-making and to build more productive relationships with others. As Joshua Freedman, CEO of Six Seconds and EQ expert, says, 'As humans we make decisions based on emotions and rationalize that decision after the fact'.

If you let your emotions slip by without reflecting on them, you are missing this valuable source of data.

CHAPTER 3: CONNECTING WITH SELF

Becoming aware of how they are running you puts you back in charge; you can navigate through your daily emotions with ease and learn to motivate and inspire others, as well as yourself. This is why I argue that connecting to self is a prerequisite to connecting with others.

Research by Tasha Eurich, an organisational psychologist and author of *Insight*, backs this up. Eurich found that managers who worked to improve their self-awareness became more effective and more promotable. They were less likely to erode trust and relationships, and more likely to build engagement and results. She argues that emotionally self-aware people are more successful, more confident, build better relationships and are more effective leaders.

This is echoed by research conducted by Fabio Sala, Principal at Organization Performance Partners and author of multiple articles. In a 2003 study of 1,214 executives and managers he found that those who failed to reach their expected level of achievement shared a common attribute: a lack of self-awareness.

I have the privilege of working with coaching clients who are ready to courageously sit with, understand and accept the emotional responses they have been bumping up against in their daily lives. The outcome? They break free from the shackles of these emotions and take back their power.

Asking you to 'look within' can bring up feelings of vulnerability. I get it. There are often parts we'd much prefer to keep hidden; we don't want to bring them to the surface for others to see. In my workshops and coaching sessions I often use what I call the beach ball metaphor in response to this. Have you ever held a beach ball underwater? If you do this for long enough it will eventually pop up and smack you in the face! This is much the same as the parts of yourself you don't like. Avoiding them can lead to career roadblocks or missed opportunities to engage your team. It's highly likely that others can see these parts even if you can't or don't want to look at them yourself.

Let me give you an example. My client – let's call her 'Ainsley' – had not been offered a promotion. She felt the person chosen for the role was less experienced and capable than her. Overall, she was better equipped and had more industry knowledge. She was upset and frustrated. While she was aware of this, she was less attentive to the bigger impact this decision had had on her behaviour. She had become blunt and overtly direct in her approach. It wasn't until she stopped and reflected that she realised her frustration and disappointment was seeping into her daily interactions with key stakeholders. She was coming across as offensive at times, they told her. Once she saw this, instead of trying to push away the emotions she felt at not being selected for promotion, she stopped and reflected on them. She recognised the level of self-doubt this had caused. Was she good enough? Would she ever have the opportunity to progress at her current organisation? Why had she not been chosen? Taking the time to process her emotions, gave her the space to start to reflect more objectively. She asked for feedback to understand where she could continue to develop, thus positioning herself for when the next promotional opportunity arose. Those around her noticed the difference in her behaviour and demeanour, and they acknowledged the strength of character it took to learn from her recent setback. She pursued opportunities to develop, adapt and evolve and, in response, they saw her as courageous and willing to learn.

I've included a few more case studies at the end of this chapter to illustrate the power of emotional self-awareness and regulation, but first let's take a look at emotional regulation.

Emotional regulation

Your feelings are a normal part of being human. Your behaviours and actions are a choice.

Think back to a time you reacted or were 'triggered' by something someone said or did, or by an event out of your control. Having replayed the event in the cool light of day you wish you'd responded differently. These situations can leave you feeling disempowered and disorientated, and it can be toxic for the people around you. Emotional self-awareness empowers you to recognise the trigger and respond differently. This is called emotional regulation.

Emotional regulation helps you remain calm and composed in difficult situations. It helps you avoid emotional overwhelm, which is likely to lead to reactionary behaviour, and help you to respond appropriately. It doesn't mean you are suppressing your emotions, it means you are not letting them take over.

Let's take a moment to look at how our emotions work in the brain.

The amygdala is a primal area of our brain responsible for our fight-flight response. It is designed to support us in times of threat. For our cavemen ancestors, this kept them alive. If a lion was approaching, they did not need to think: they needed to react, and quickly! Today, we react in much the same way when we feel threatened. Yet the threats are not generally life endangering. For instance, if our boss yells at us, or a friend teases us, our amygdala instinctively reacts, bypassing the cognitive part of our brain. Unfortunately, our initial response is not always the 'correct' one. That experience of having a negative interaction, only to cool down later and wish you had responded differently, is an amygdala hijack, a term coined by EQ expert Daniel Goleman. Emotional regulation can help you avoid the hijack.

By taking the time to pause sufficiently and breath, when we have an emotional response to something, we enable the 'thinking' part of our brain to come on board.

CHAPTER 3: CONNECTING WITH SELF

This means utilising our cerebral cortex, our cognition, giving us the opportunity to offer a more thoughtful response. In short, the emotional and thinking parts of our brain start to work in unison.

This is what I am referring to as 'emotional regulation'. You are aware of the emotion you are experiencing *and* you are able to regulate your response accordingly. Your emotional and cognitive states are working together. And the more you can develop emotional self-awareness, the greater your ability to understand and modulate your emotional responses.

With a dedicated, ongoing practice and a structured self-reflective process, you will start to bring your neocortex online in tough situations. I'd like to use myself as an example here.

My partner and son are surfers. Wanting to join them in the water rather than sitting on the beach and watching them, I decided to take up body boarding. All was going well until one particular outing when my partner suggested I stay close to the shore as there was a big swell. As I dived under one wave, then the next, I was enjoying the view until, quite suddenly, I was dragged at speed by a rip into the section of heavy waves. As I splashed around in the water, trying to navigate the large waves crashing over my head, my partner and son came to my rescue. My partner, a seasoned surfer, yelled clear instructions over the crashing waves, 'Paddle with me into shore'. Off she went and was standing on the beach in 30 seconds. I just didn't have the strength or the understanding of how to navigate my way through crashing waves and rip-fuelled water; I was out of my depth. I started to panic, which effected my ability to breath. I paddled wildly but I wasn't getting anywhere. My partner pointed directions from the beach and my son stayed close, talking calmly to me, reaffirming I would be ok. I knew I needed to get control over my rising anxiety and the negative thoughts that were swirling in my head. I paused. I stopped trying to get anywhere. I took a deep breath, then another and another, until I felt myself calm down. I told myself this is a new situation but if I follow guidance and take my time, I will be ok. I looked up, I breathed deeply, I surveyed the scene. You can do this, I told myself, just take your time. With that, I was able to absorb instructions, and my son and I paddled to shore.

Although I've never lived this story down, I was able to regulate my emotions in an environment I found highly stressful. You can too.

Connecting to self at a glance

What a gift it is to have the tools to explore ourselves, to know ourselves, and to be present and connected with ourselves.

This is the path to self-worth, to finding our authentic

CHAPTER 3: CONNECTING WITH SELF

voice, to freedom of choice and a place of calm. To clarity and direction, and a sense of achievement.

And once you can do this for yourself, you are able to do it with others.

This is why connecting to self is at the foundation of The Pinnacle of Presence framework.

Connecting to self in action

Let's look at how this plays out in some case studies of my clients (names changed.)

Ava

Ava came into our first session wanting something to change. She was apprehensive but open, knowing it was time to let her guard down, time to stop exerting power with her peers and management team. For years she had worked under a boss she didn't get along with. This boss, she told me, used bullying tactics. Ava responded to this in kind and over time developed a habit of being aggressive with those around her. She earned a reputation for being difficult.

Finally, her boss moved on. Ava had her opportunity for a new start. Her new boss arrived and showed her nothing but respect, empowering her to make decisions and manage her team as she saw fit. Her boss listened, he empathised, he supported, he set clear direction and purpose. This stopped Ava in her tracks, 'I've become the person that mistreated and bullied me. I've become my ex-boss. People fear me. I don't want to be that person'.

Ava had connected to self. She had recognised that her way of being in the world was no longer working. Not for her, nor those around her. She was empowered to change.

Luca

Luca, a general manager with 20 years' experience, is about to head into a tough meeting. He knows that many of his peers are not aligned with his direction on a particular project he is leading. He knows the organisation is looking for him to get an outcome, and quickly. Before he enters the room he pauses. He is aware of a well-known mindfulness practice – STOP – and takes a moment to practice it quietly. STOP is an acronym: Stop. Take a moment. Observe what you're thinking, feeling, doing. Proceed.

CHAPTER 3: CONNECTING WITH SELF

This exercise, which took Luca less than ten seconds to complete, is one he's become practised at as he knows it supports him in feeling grounded and at ease. He smiles and enters the room with presence.

By Luca taking this moment to check in with his emotional state, he is able to get a sense of what he needs to refine within himself. He makes any necessary changes to his thinking patterns, his posture, how he's breathing, his body language and so on, and then he lets go of anything that is not serving him or relevant to the outcome he's seeking. As a result, he is able to actively turn his attention to the coming agenda.

Joe

In Joe's initial coaching session he shared how he had a history of losing control, getting angry and demonstrating frustration at work. In a recent incident this had escalated to the point he was shouting at his manager and making derogatory comments towards her. Joe's organisation had stepped in at this point and scheduled a mediation session between Joe and his boss.

Hearing the impact of his behaviour directly from his colleague during the mediation session was the impetus that motivated Joe to change his behaviour. Rather than continuing to blame others around him, he looked inwards, working to understand what was driving his reactions and subsequent behaviour. He wanted to break the cycle and agreed to undertake an emotional intelligence coaching program. As he did the work of introspection, he started to see **patterns**. In particular he noticed his anger would surface when he felt he wasn't being treated with respect. From there he was able to **observe himself** having the reaction, and could **choose a different response**, rather than react on autopilot, as he would have done in the past. As a result, he transformed his relationships with his manager and other co-workers.

Genevieve

Genevieve came into her first session feeling very demotivated. She had loved her job for a long time, but was at the point where she was considering quitting and taking another role. This wasn't what she wanted. Not really. She wanted to reignite her passion for her current role.

CHAPTER 3: CONNECTING WITH SELF

She took the time in our coaching sessions to dig deep, to challenge her negative spiral. She started to recognise patterns. The most telling being how she had lost connection with her geographically dispersed team, and just how central connection had been to her motivation. She also saw the possibilities that would open up if she reconnected with her team out in the field. Rather than having to come up with all the solutions herself, her team would be able to share their ideas and provide invaluable input.

Until this point she hadn't stopped and taken time to reflect on this. She'd been moving through her days and hadn't understood how much this mattered to her. As the end of the year drew to a close, she built more time in her diary for the following year to focus on connecting with her team. She spent time learning how to connect and collaborate virtually, as well as face to face and her confidence grew in this space. Her energy returned, she was revitalised.

Developing emotional self-awareness and regulation

Developing self-awareness is an ongoing process and takes work. Human beings are like onions. Remove one layer and there's a whole new layer beneath. The key is to develop a regular self-reflective habit.

It's like going to the gym. Everyone can talk about getting fit and healthy, but if you don't do the work of lifting those dumbbells or running on the treadmill *consistently*, nothing will shift. Instead it is the regular, tiny nudges that will ultimately transform you. You may not see the benefits overnight, in the same way you don't see the benefits of regular exercise on a day to day basis. However, as you compare yourself *over time*, you will clearly see the difference.

A self-reflective habit: the pathway to emotional self-awareness and regulation

Step 1. Observe and name your emotions
External stimuli (an event) can generate unconscious thoughts, feelings, and actions. At this point you have a *choice*. You can:

A. Pause and reflect (observe your reaction), or

B. React (not consciously choosing how to respond).

By choosing option A you are on the path to emotional self-awareness.

Observe your reaction with *no judgement* (I do understand this is sometimes easier said than done. Practice. Be gentle on yourself).

Ask what am I thinking, feeling, doing?

Name the emotion.

Ask yourself what bodily sensations you recognise, for example a fast pulse, or the tightening of your throat. (See the Interoception section below in 'Further exercises to support emotional self-awareness and regulation'.)

Step 2. Understand linkages or patterns of behaviour
Work to understand the reaction and driver of the emotion (i.e. recognise the pattern). To do this:
1. Once you notice a feeling, think about how you are reacting to that feeling.
2. By capturing that reaction, you can then start to see if there are any recurring themes.

Often, we react to the same things over and over again, unconsciously. By stopping and reflecting, *without judgement*, you may start to see links (i.e. certain situations or events) that cause us to react in the same way each time.

Make a note of these reflections either in a journal, in the notes section of your phone, or somewhere that suits you. It could look like:

Event:
Date:
I thought:

I felt:

I did:

Or draw a picture if you would rather not think about it too cognitively. Review these reflections periodically and look for themes and linkages. By understanding these links, you will start to recognise your patterns of behaviour, and have greater insight into what is causing you to react in these situations.

As an example, refer to the case study of Joe above. In his coaching program, Joe shared, 'When I felt myself having an emotional reaction to something, I would make a quick note of the context and what I was saying to myself. Over time I noticed that I would say "that person doesn't respect me". I came to see this was an old thought pattern I'd created from my childhood experience. Now, when that thought comes up, I'm gentle with myself and say "thanks for sharing" and I don't let it impact how I respond to the person in front of me, in the here and now'.

Consider making this a nightly activity, or set an alarm for a suitable time. Spend 15 minutes reflecting on your day and run through the various behaviours and actions that stand out to you.

Did you have a negative reaction? Did you interact in a way that you aren't proud of, or regret? What can you learn from these experiences?

A regular practice helps you set up a reflective habit to develop emotional self-awareness.

CHAPTER 3: CONNECTING WITH SELF

Feedback from others

It isn't always easy to know when you aren't emotionally self-aware. Your own behaviour can be a blind spot. By gathering feedback from others and comparing this with your own reflection, you can start to see if there are any gaps in your understanding of your behaviour and how this is actually perceived by others. Significant gaps are likely to be limiting your performance and impacting on your relationships. We will cover this in much more detail in Chapter 5.

Feedback from your body

You experience emotions in your body, so when emotions are charged within you, you experience bodily sensations such as your pulse quickening, your muscles tensing, or your breath changing.

To loosen the grip this emotional response has on you, follow these steps:
- Notice your bodily reaction (this is called interoception – perception of internal signals in your body).
- Label the emotion (this is called emotional literacy).
- Take time to understand where this emotion comes from.

Exercises to quickly ground you in the present when you're busy

STOP
Stop
Take a break
Observe what you are thinking, feeling, doing
Proceed

Mindful eating or walking
Or washing up! Any activity can be used. Suspend attention in other areas and focus purely on that activity.

Five senses
The goal is to notice something that you are currently experiencing through each of your senses. What is the one thing you can see, feel, hear, smell and taste?

Breathing
Conscious breathing is so often underutilised, yet a powerful way for us to regulate our emotions.

Breathing techniques, such as box breathing and diaphragmatic breathing, allow you to activate your parasympathetic nervous system (the calming response in your body), as opposed to your autonomic nervous system (the fight/flight response).

CHAPTER 3: CONNECTING WITH SELF

Making bodily changes
For instance, you can slow your pace of speech, utilise more pauses, or slow the pace of your walk.

Proactive measures

Finally, take the time to consider what steps you can incorporate into your day to support ongoing emotional self-awareness and regulation. Two examples are physical activity and meditation.

It is much easier to emotionally regulate when you are taking care of your physical health. If regular exercise, a healthy diet and sufficient sleep aren't part of your daily routine, I encourage you to find ways to incorporate them. This will also support your mental health and wellbeing.

I have shared a couple of mindfulness activities above. You may also like to consider a meditation practice. There are a number of meditation apps you can download and try. Smiling Mind, Headspace and Ten Percent are three such examples.

What's next?

Having developed the capacity to connect with self, we now turn our attention to developing Inner Presence.

CHAPTER 4

INNER PRESENCE

Enormous energy is set free when we finally drop the mask, when we dare to be fully ourselves.

FREDERIC LALOUX
REINVENTING ORGANIZATIONS

I define Inner Presence as: *Being self-empowered to fully accept and believe in yourself, confident to show others the real you.*

Understanding yourself and being comfortable with the real you makes your life easier and puts you in control. Accepting all parts of yourself leads to self-worth and inner confidence, which in turn allows you to stand powerfully in who you are and face what lies before you.

Think of the best moments of your life: the times you have felt the most alive, most joyful, most fully yourself, and 'in the zone'. This is your 'best' self. Inner Presence helps you bring that person to the challenges you face today.

It gives you confidence in the toughest of situations. It empowers you to be the best version of you. It is the bedrock of being a leader in these complex times.

The key elements of bringing your Inner Presence to life are:
- having a personal vision of your ideal future state to work towards
- knowing your core values and being true to them
- embracing your uniqueness, your strengths and areas for development.

By understanding these elements you will be clear on when you are being the best and most authentic version of you, your best self, and when you're not.

No doubt life will throw challenges your way, and you may feel, at times, that you are swimming in the deep end, but by focusing on the above elements, you can feel confident you are doing the absolute best you can with the skills you have. You are showing up and giving it your best go, with Inner Presence.

Personal vision of your ideal future state

Our ability to be our most authentic, best self is limited if we don't have a clear vision for ourselves and our future. Until we have clearly determined *what we stand for* and what we aspire to be, we will lack clarity on *how we want to behave at our best*.

CHAPTER 4: INNER PRESENCE

As a leader, you know it's important to set the stage for your direct reports in understanding your team's vision and how their work contributes to the bigger picture. As Martin Luther King said, 'If you want to move people, it has to be toward a vision that's positive for them, that taps important values, that gets them something they desire and it has to be presented in a compelling way so that they feel inspired to follow'. This is empowering for your team; it can be empowering for you too.

My stepfather, Cliff, came from a very poor background. He grew up in a small house with two bedrooms, in a family of nine. He received no encouragement to aspire or dream for a brighter future. Instead he was expected to leave school, earn an income and bring it home. Money was the main objective. Nothing else mattered, simply because there was so little of it.

Within the school environment he and his siblings were known as a family of poor social class, and no one expected them to achieve academically. Cliff accepted this assumption at a young age. Going home to a poor environment, with no encouragement, served as reinforcement.

As he turned 18, there came a turning point. His best friend encouraged him to take the entrance test to become a nurse. He passed. 'It dawned on me,' he told me, 'that my childhood didn't have to define me, and that I was more intelligent than I realised'.

Cliff started to envisage a different future: one that

was a far cry from his past. He saw possibilities he didn't know existed. And this ideal future state directed the choices he made in the present moment.

He became motivated to take on further academic study, knowing that with qualifications he would reach a higher status. Given his childhood experience, social standing and the financial benefits of promotion, to enable him to support his family, were key drivers.

He was propelled by his core values: learning, drive, status, optimism and compassion.

He ultimately worked his way through Britain's NHS system to achieve the role of Director of Nursing Services. He visualised his future, lived by his values and created a life for himself that was unrecognisable from his past.

One of Cliff's favourite quotes is by American social reformer, abolitionist and writer Frederick Douglass: 'You are not judged by the height you have risen, but from the depth you have climbed'. His vision for his future motivated him to climb a very long way.

Imagine you're on a sailing ship in Sydney Harbour and a storm hits (in your working environment this could be a crisis, an unexpected deadline or negative outburst from someone around you). You are confident in your sailing abilities and are playing to your strengths. You are clear on your vision, which is to reach the Opera House by sunset. You have no control over what the elements will do and how they will impact you. Yet, by

CHAPTER 4: INNER PRESENCE

being clear about your personal vision you have a direction and the necessary motivation to navigate yourself, moment by moment. You're confidently doing all you can with what you have. Having a personal vision for your life works the same way.

Having clarity on your personal vision, you are more likely to be motivated to move towards it. As an example, athletes often visualise themselves winning the race to propel them towards success.

I recently worked with a client who was fatigued. He was keen to build greater vitality in his life. He wanted to stop allowing work to take over his life, to no longer work in the evenings and over the weekend (as did his family). This was a long-standing habit and one that took real effort to break. What made the difference? He took the time to really pause and reflect on what his *ideal future* looked like. He lifted his eyes up from the day-to-day work and looked over the horizon to visualise what was next. This excited him. His ideal future state included his ability to sustain momentum, his fitness levels and overall health.

By switching his lens from current state to future state, he was able to motivate himself to change how he was acting in the present.

Of course, at times, deadlines needed to be met. This is unavoidable, and it was important for him to keep a 'here and now' perspective. However, now he had options. He could choose: short term lens or long term lens. By arming himself with his long-term vision he was able to maintain sustained momentum. He felt empowered. The quality and quantity of his sleep improved, as did his vitality and enthusiasm, and he was able to start enjoying time with his family again.

Being intentional in creating your ideal future state will set you up with the right mindset. Imagine it's the Friday before you're about to go on your dream holiday. You have a huge amount of work on your desk, but you're leaving tomorrow so you are feeling in a great mood. Your vision of the future is motivating you to get through those piles of work.

Visualising your ideal future affects who you are being in the present moment. A personal vision changes how we view our current reality. Instead of seeing this as fixed, we pause, and look up, out towards an exciting destination we've imagined for ourselves. One that motivates and inspires us. The person we are being today shifts, and with more energy and clarity we proceed.

Core values

A client of mine, let's call her 'Orla', had lost her way. The demands of her daily role had intruded into all other areas of her life. Her focus had become solely work-centric and she was frustrated. She had a sense of foreboding, knowing this was not what she wanted,

CHAPTER 4: INNER PRESENCE

yet as the list of work priorities got longer, she was doggedly determined to meet them. So, she continued on. Her frustration grew and others noticed. By the time we started to work together, Orla was miserable and confused about how to navigate her way forward with success. She wanted to feel energised and enthused again – and confident in herself. She just didn't know how. For someone so capable, smart and professionally successful, this confusion and self-doubt left her feeling vulnerable and frustrated. This is a common story.

She had lost connection with her inner barometer: her core values.

Having a clear sense of purpose – a personal vision – and aligning this work with your core values gives you confidence that you are on the right track. Or if you aren't on the right track, it gives you clarity on where to focus your attention.

Values act as your guiding compass.

Mahatma Gandhi, one of my personal heroes, stood for peace and nonviolence. He famously said, 'Be the change you want to see,' meaning if you want to live in a different world, act that way. This was a clear articulation of his values, and he lived according to them.

A story I've often read about Gandhi (although I do not know where it originated from) is of a woman bringing her son to Gandhi because he was eating too much sugar. She wanted Gandhi to ask her son to stop. Gandhi asked her to bring her son back in two days.

She brought him back, and Gandhi said to the son, 'Stop eating sugar'. The mother replied, 'Why could you not say that two days ago?' Gandhi replied, 'Because I needed to stop eating it first'.

Your core values support you in making the right choices for you, allowing you to prioritise based on what is important to you.

Let's consider a couple of examples. If you are clear that *health* is your number one core value, yet you've worked twelve hour days for the past two weeks, leaving no time to exercise and get out into the fresh air, then you can be clear you are not living your life according to your values. By contrast, if *family* is your number one value and, despite running a time-critical project, you have made time to eat with your family four out of the past five working days, you are more likely to be living according to your values.

Please understand I am not referring to organisational values here. While these are important, I'm focusing on your core, personal values. These values will be driving your behaviour whether you are aware of them or not. The more clarity you have on what these are, the more easily you can drive yourself forward, aligned with what is most important to you. That said, I encourage you to choose a workplace whose organisational values align with your personal values.

Returning to Orla, as she and I reflected on her life to date – what had shaped her, her beliefs and assumptions,

CHAPTER 4: INNER PRESENCE

her personal drivers and key motivators – her level of self-awareness grew.

> She paused and reflected from a broader perspective, across her timeline and across all areas of her life. She took a bird's eye view of what mattered to her most. With this clarity she saw just how inconsistently she had been living according to her values. This is easy to do. She had become pulled along by other people's agendas and a need to achieve results at all costs. Others I work with are magnetised towards the next big thing, such as career progression and promotion, or the desire to please. Whatever the reason, we always know at our core when we are moving away from or not consistently living our values. We become frustrated or demotivated.
>
> Through our sessions Orla came to recognise this, so she committed to running any decision through her values lens. She worked hard to act and make choices according to her values. This included a commitment to switching off and spending time in the evenings with her partner and daughter. She committed to working from home once per week. She started exercising again, she returned to yoga and she booked regular time in the diary to spend with extended family

and friends. She started to decline meetings and empowered her team to attend instead. She accepted that she was not going to get everything done on her to-do list. She learnt to prioritise and to be comfortable with that.

Being clear about her values gave her freedom to be true to herself and to feel confident she was always moving in a direction that was right for her. She had her own guiding compass. With this, her energy returned. While she could not control the external circumstances, or what was asked of her, she always had the best mentor by her side to help her make her decisions: herself.

Does she always get this right? No. Does anyone? No. But with a commitment to regular reflection and self-awareness she can bring herself back in focus time and time again.

Live your life according to your values, and you will live a life of courage, confidence and one that is true to you.

CHAPTER 4: INNER PRESENCE

Your uniqueness

Often when I ask my clients 'what is your leadership style?' or 'give me three words to describe your leadership style' they aren't clear on the response. They tell me they model their leader's behaviour or the behaviour of other leaders around them.

While it is valuable to observe others and pick qualities you'd like to emulate, I encourage you to find a style that fits you, one that is uniquely yours. Don't try to be the leader you think you *should* be, but be the leader you want to be, that you're inspired to be. Others will know if you are not being *real*, and it will come across as fake.

I recently coached a female leader who worked in a predominantly male environment. She was relatively new in her senior leadership role and was working hard to manage anxiety. The root cause for this was her lack of clarity around what sort of leader she should be in her given context. She didn't have many female role models, was not loud or overly extraverted (qualities she had thought were necessary). She questioned how she could engage and galvanise the respect of her peers and employees. Taking the time to pause and reflect on and understanding her own beliefs, attitudes and values allowed her to accept where she was, as opposed to fighting it. With this acceptance came the realisation that it was okay to fully and genuinely show up as herself. She got to work on building her own leadership style. This new level of self-awareness led to self-empowerment and, ultimately, to the creation of an engaged and culturally strong workforce.

Understanding your own unique and authentic leadership style and acting accordingly is empowering – both for you and for the people around you.

Strengths and areas for development

To understand what makes you unique, it is important to be clear about your strengths and weaknesses (or areas for development, as I prefer to call them).

Martin Seligman is an American psychologist and author who is commonly referred to as the father of positive psychology. He argues, you are at your best when you are using your strengths to meet your biggest challenges.

Taking the time to reflect on your strengths supports you in understanding who you are at the core. Exploring and talking about your strengths brings them to life. I have watched clients time and again become self-empowered as they hear themselves say their strengths out loud. They become more aware of them and are able to bring them more regularly into their daily life and interactions. This builds their self-esteem and inner confidence, which helps them to interact with authenticity.

At the same time, it is important to keep in mind that strengths can be overused. Overplayed strengths can derail leaders.

CHAPTER 4: INNER PRESENCE

Let's consider 'Jim'. Jim was a client of mine working in a senior leadership position within the healthcare sector during the beginning of COVID-19 pandemic. He was under immense pressure and his landscape was changing rapidly. As he navigated daily challenges with his team, he was confident that he was playing to his strengths of being decisive, caring and courageous.

At the same time he was aware of his tendency to overuse his strength of decisiveness: 'I make quick decisions, and I adjust and modify as we keep moving. While this can be a strength, I am aware that my continual corrections can cause increased stress for the team. I can see that my strength backfires at times'. With this awareness, Jim made a conscious effort to explicitly provide context for his team and explain his rationale. He also sought input from the team as decisions were made and adjusted. With this, he was able to garner buy-in from the team and, with this, he saw engagement and motivation soar.

It's important to leverage your strengths wherever possible. It's also important to be aware of where you need to bridge gaps that may be limiting your potential. Understanding your areas for development that can help you move closer to operating at your 'best' self is an opportunity to learn, adapt and evolve.

Learning is key in our complex times. And as we learn we make mistakes, and as we make mistakes we learn, and we grow.

When it comes to both strengths and development gaps, self-denial limits self-awareness and growth so, as well as taking the time to self-reflect, also make it a regular practice to ask for and listen to genuine feedback.

A coaching client who is highly successful in her field, recently shared this as she completed her coaching program:

> 'As I've taken time out to self-reflect and work through the coaching process, I've continued to find areas to develop myself. I've come to realise I have been accepting mediocrity and the status quo. Had I not taken time out to look inwards, re-evaluating my values, strengths, and developmental gaps, this would not have come to the surface.'

She subsequently went on to apply and be accepted for a promotion: something she had not considered before re-establishing a self-reflective process.

Dynamic and ever shifting

Inner Presence isn't a permanent state. It's a moment-by-moment dynamic and ever-shifting space. Different contexts and people lead you to act in varying ways. Knowing what is at the core of you will keep you

CHAPTER 4: INNER PRESENCE

real in whatever circumstances head your way.

Your experience changes in different contexts and situations. One moment you may get fantastic feedback, and in the next your work is criticised. Hence the need for Inner Presence. Inner Presence is what is going on within you as you navigate the world, go about your daily life and interact with others. The world is not consistent, and it doesn't always show up as you expect. Inner Presence is something you will always need to tune into.

Ask: what do I need to tell myself or remind myself of in this moment? What will serve me?

As Brené Brown writes in her best-selling book *Dare to Lead*, 'When we define ourselves by what everyone thinks, it's hard to be brave'. On the other hand, she also points out, 'When we stop caring about what *anyone* thinks, we're too armoured for authentic connection'. To find middle ground, I recommend you consider two or three people whose opinions *really* matter to you and ask them to give you honest feedback when necessary. These need to be people who don't just agree with what you have to say, but will call you out if they think you've acted inappropriately. Choose people who will have your back and are willing and courageous enough to be honest with you when necessary.

Some of my coaching clients say, 'I'm the same wherever I go. I don't change'. While we may be the same person at our core, we need to show up differently depending on the context. For instance, if you were waiting on some test results from your heart surgeon and turned up at his or her rooms to receive them, would you be comfortable if they were wearing board shorts and thongs?

Are you the same person with your nearest and dearest as you are with your intimate partner or your mother, or the Dalai Lama?

Would you demonstrate the same behaviours with an employee you are delivering bad news to as you would when celebrating a team member's sales win? While you are the same person, how you engage with others will differ. We will explore this further in Chapter 5 when we review Leadership Presence.

Take a moment to note any differences in your behaviour across situations involving various people. For instance, think about how you behave with a friend and then with your boss, when you're bored or when you're stressed, or in a regular weekly meeting versus a moment of crisis. Become aware of the differences in the ways you interact.

You may feel challenged by the idea that Inner Presence is a moment-by-moment experience – that you can't just tick a box and move on. It is being intentional in each moment about who you are and what you offer. With small nudges and tweaks you will gain clarity on your Inner Presence.

CHAPTER 4: INNER PRESENCE

A personal story of self-reflection and meaning

Two years ago I was diagnosed with an autoimmune condition. This came as quite a shock to me. I had always taken my health as a given. I ate healthily, I exercised. I was lucky enough to have great family and friends and I led a balanced life.

Prior to the diagnosis I had experienced a range of painful symptoms, yet, despite great care from my GP and appointments with various specialists, no one could tell me what was wrong. It was a frightening time, and it was frustrating.

By the time I got the answer, I was spent: fatigued physically, mentally and emotionally. Then I had to get my head around living with a condition and a range of symptoms that, while could be relieved, could not be resolved. I fought against it. I stopped sleeping. I battled on. Until I couldn't.

In the week leading up to the Christmas of 2018, at a time when I 'should' have been excited about the festive season and spending time with my family, I actually felt depleted and bereft.

I booked myself into a hotel with a spa for the weekend. I gave myself a silent retreat! I went for facials, I read, I sat with myself.

During that weekend I came to a realisation that I needed to accept the 'new normal' of my life. One in which I needed to monitor my health by listening to my body and mind, taking time to stop and rest when I needed to (instead of continually driving myself). I also got back in touch with all that I had, rather than focusing on what had been taken from me.

I saw just how much I'd been giving myself a hard time, all the negative self-talk, all the times I'd beaten myself up for 'getting' the disease, unconsciously blaming myself. Illogical but, nonetheless, true. I also saw the negative impact of this mindset on the people closest to me: my partner, son and parents. This wasn't who I wanted to be for them, or for myself. I had a life to live.

Recognising the negative self-talk took the power away from it. It diffused it. I chose self-compassion and self-care instead.

By no longer fighting against my diagnosis and the situation I found myself in, I was able to sit with it and feel the impact of the past few years. I acknowledged it, and it hurt. A lot. Did I feel better immediately? No. But it was the first step towards the acceptance of my new normal. I started to see a new way forward.

I made the decision to leave my permanent employment role, despite loving the people I worked with, and focus full-time on my own coaching and consulting business. I knew the number one question I needed to continually ask myself when making choices about how I live my life was: does it give me vitality?

This meant finding a way to focus purely on the types

CHAPTER 4: INNER PRESENCE

of work I love – the projects and assignments that light me up and energise me. And to say no to work that didn't. A life that gave me the gaps I needed to take time out to be in nature – to go for a walk, inhale the ocean air, watch the birds – activities that breathe life into me, and keep me grounded and present.

This is what allows me to be fully present when I'm with my clients, my family and my friends.

Without the diagnosis, I may not have had the courage to take the necessary steps to make this happen. It was the tipping point. And for this I'm extraordinarily grateful.

It's important to mention too that this wasn't just a one-time only solution. I have to practise these steps constantly. And I really mean constantly. I find myself doing too much at times and having to stop and recharge. The difference now is that I don't give myself a hard time about switching gears.

Why do I share this personal story? To illustrate that while I know the 'how' of Inner Presence, it isn't the same as actually practising it.

It isn't easy, it takes work. But ultimately, the outcome of doing the work of Inner Presence proves more fruitful than self-denial. It can be liberating to take your power back.

Make your own choices based on what is of value to you, having weighed up the consequences, no matter what is thrown your way.

Inner Presence at a glance

Inner Presence is about embracing yourself, in each and every moment, finding ways to connect with the real you and celebrating your uniqueness. Talking to yourself in a way that serves you, and that empowers you, especially in times of high stakes and/or stress.

Reminding yourself of your vision, values and strengths, especially during challenging times and tough conversations, will help you talk positively to yourself and express yourself in ways that feel, and are perceived by others, as genuine. It will help you act as your best self, generating confidence in your abilities and belief in yourself, which in turn will help you take action towards what matters. The more you practice this, the more empowered you will feel. It is a self-perpetuating loop.

With Inner Presence you can be confident in the toughest situations; this is the bedrock of being a leader in this complex world.

I'm not asking you to be someone you are not. I'm asking you to focus on how you can be the best version of *you*. This allows you to chart your own course and not be at the mercy of others or any situation that comes hurtling your way. You can choose to *respond* rather than *react* in these moments.

Understanding and accepting all aspects of yourself, even those you don't like very much will generate your sense of self-worth and, ultimately, inner confidence.

This is not a one-time event. This takes nudges and tweaks in each and every moment. Cut yourself some slack when you need to. You are not perfect. No one is. Don't forget you're human too. Go easy on yourself.

Developing Inner Presence can feel counterintuitive when you have a lot on your plate, but my clients have repeatedly shown that investing now supports them in having more time in the future.

Take this first step seriously, it's the foundation of profound change.

Inner Presence learning and development plan

Now it's time for you to create a learning and development plan to work and refine your Inner Presence, with a sense of ease, feeling grounded and remaining confident about who you are and how to get there.

There are three steps:
1. Define your personal vision of an ideal future state
2. Identify your core values
3. Conduct a courageous self-assessment to recognise your strengths and areas for development.

Step 1. Define your personal vision of an ideal future state

Reflect on your life stories
Our lives are complex and to make meaning from our experience, we create stories. Our reality becomes the stories we tell ourselves. Reflecting on these narratives gives us insight into what is important to us and why.

Carve out time to reflect on key events in your life and what you made them mean. How has this contributed to the person you have become, the person you aspire to be, your strengths, motivation and the values you hold dear? As you reflect on what you've captured here, consider how this informs the ideal future you want to create: your personal vision.

Write a letter
Write a letter to your 90-year-old self. Tell them what you hope to achieve and who you hope to be in life, your aspirations and dreams. What lights you up and excites you? And why. You cannot get this wrong – it is your ideal future state. Just write and see what unfolds. Create. Play.

As you write, consider:
- What are my dreams and aspirations? (Work, personal or in any other area important to you.)
- What do I want to be known for?
- What gives me energy?

CHAPTER 4: INNER PRESENCE

Step 2. Identify your core values

Do you have a clear sense of your own values, and do you act in a way consistent with those values? Does your work fit well with your personal values?

To give you a sense of your values, ask yourself:
- What really lights me up and excites me?
- How would I describe my perfect day?
- If money wasn't an issue for me, how would I spend my day?

This may not be a new concept to many, yet it is surprising how many of us don't live our lives according to our values.

Consider the following questions:
1. Are you clear on what is important to you?
2. What are the top five most important areas of your life?
3. Do you devote time to these five areas?

Getting clear on your values
Listed below are common examples of values. These may not all be relevant for you. This is a personal exercise, so take the time to reflect on what personal values are important to you, not anyone else.

Begin by picking broad themes and then check for any that are interrelated. For instance, you may choose 'family', 'love', and 'connection' as potential values. When you reflect further, you may feel that 'family' covers each of these. Or perhaps 'connection' does. Pick a word that resonates best for you. As an example, I love hiking and this is something I do regularly with my son. Hiking, for me, represents 'health', 'nature', 'family', and 'connection'. All of these values are significant for me, which explains why hiking is so meaningful to me – it fits across a number of my core values.

These are some common values to consider, or feel free to pick your own:

- family
- friends
- health
- spirituality
- career
- fun
- personal growth
- financial security
- connection
- balance
- challenge
- curiosity
- excellence
- knowledge
- wellbeing

Now get this down to five broad themes and make a note about what this value means for you. For instance,

CHAPTER 4: INNER PRESENCE

'family' could mean something for you which is quite different for me.

If you are struggling to whittle this down to five, imagine you are in a boat and there is a hole in it. The boat is starting to sink, you are close to shore. You need to get rid of weight quickly. Which values would you be willing to throw overboard to avoid sinking and which ones would you hold vehemently onto?

Keep asking:
- What is important to me?
- What do I care about?
- What do I want to work towards?

Another way to approach this is to imagine opening five bank accounts and labelling them with each of your top five values.
- Are you investing equally into each account?
- If not, why not?

If you don't keep an eye on these investments, what will these accounts look like in five years?

Will you see any returns on your investments? For instance, if one of your values is 'family' and you do not make any investment into that relationship (i.e. take the time out of work to have dinner together, talk with one another, have fun together etc.), what will that 'bank account' look like in five years?

Once you have clarity on your values you are equipped

to make decisions and set direction that is in alignment. For instance, if offered a new role, you can ask yourself, 'will this role allow me to stay true to my values?' As you make any decision, consider if it fits with your values.

Step 3. Conduct a courageous self-assessment to recognise your strengths and areas for development

Here are a few questions to consider to identify your strengths:
- When do you feel most 'in the zone'?
- Where do you excel?
- What natural talents have you refined into strengths over time?

SWOT analysis is also a useful model I use with many of my clients:

Strengths
- What skills and talents do you demonstrate?
- Have you received feedback regarding particular strengths?
- Think back over your day. What gave you 'yes' or 'up' energy? Does this highlight strengths and skills?

Weaknesses
- Have you received feedback about areas that need improvement?
- Where do you feel you lack ability or skills?

- Think back over your day. What gave you 'no' or 'low' energy? Does this highlight gaps or areas needing development?

Opportunities
- What do your strengths and skills offer in terms of opportunities?
- What strengths could you capitalise on?
- In what ways could you be leveraging your strengths? For instance, perhaps you can join an SME (subject-matter expert) group at work where your skillset would be valued?

Threats
- Do any of your weaknesses open up potential threats?
- What obstacles do you need to overcome?

Having completed these exercises, take the time to capture final reflections. Use the Inner Presence Action Plan as a guide.

INNER PRESENCE ACTION PLAN: BRINGING IT ALL TOGETHER

My personal vision
Write one statement that encapsulates key points

_____

_____

My core values

1. _____
2. _____
3. _____
4. _____
5. _____

Top 3 strengths _____

1. _____

_____

2. _____

_____

3. _____

CHAPTER 4: INNER PRESENCE

I plan to continue leveraging these strengths by:

_____

_____

_____

Three key areas for development
What does success look like as I achieve my goal/ develop in this area?

1. _____

_____

2. _____

_____

3. _____

_____

Emotional self-awareness and regulation
What do I need to be aware of? What triggers may lead me to react instead of respond? And what steps can I take to manage this?(Refer to your responses in Chapter 3).

1. _____

_____

2. _____

_____

3. _____

_____

Actions I will take to develop and refine my Inner Presence

1. _____

_____

2. _____

_____

3. _____

_____

What's next?

Next, we'll explore how to best project your Inner Presence outwards to build trust and connection with the people around you. Signalling to others that you have what it takes to lead. This is Leadership Presence.

CHAPTER 5

LEADERSHIP PRESENCE

Chances are, for every ten supervisors you've had throughout your career you'd probably want to work for only two or three of them again.

JIM CLIFTON & JIM HARTER
IT'S THE MANAGER

Your Inner Presence is why you do what you do. Leadership Presence is how you show up doing it.

You would have recognised Leadership Presence in others, even if you haven't been able to label or define it. It isn't about their technical skills or simply whether they produce results; it is about confidence, credibility and trust. These are the leaders that you implicitly trust to take the team in the right direction. You have confidence in their abilities, and in return they demonstrate confidence in you. These leaders have the ability to connect authentically with others, they value relationships as much as results and they lead with a balance of strength and warmth.

And now that you have started honing your reflective skills, this is the kind of leader you can be. Leadership Presence is built on your foundation of connecting to self and Inner Presence. Your ability to self-regulate, your strong sense of self, your inner confidence and calm will help you bring your best self to the role.

I define Leadership Presence as: *Projecting your Inner Presence outwards, signalling that you have what it takes to lead others.*

Leadership Presence is:
- bringing your best self to the role with inner confidence and calm
- balancing strength with warmth to build trust, connection and credibility
- reading the context and adjusting behaviours as needed.

Bringing your best self to the role of leader

In the last chapter you identified your personal vision, your core values, your strengths and development gaps. This is what you need to bring to your leadership style. (Yes, even the parts of you that need work.) Having clarity here will ensure you stand firm and are clear

CHAPTER 5: LEADERSHIP PRESENCE

in your communication, and not easily flustered when others disagree with you. You have clear boundaries and are able to say yes or no as needed.

A key part of bringing your best self is to develop your own genuine style of leadership. You can take cues from leaders you admire, but don't try to imitate someone else's leadership style, it will leave you looking fake and will not build trust, confidence and credibility. Instead, embody your Inner Presence (why you do what you do) and bring your genuine and best self to the role. It is an inside-out approach.

Having become clear on the 'inner' component, it is equally important to be clear on how you define your role as leader (as distinct from other roles you play in your life), how you want to be perceived in this role, and to be clear that how others perceive you is what you intended. You can then feel confident that your inner confidence and calm will be seen by others appropriately, and you will build credibility and trust.

Balancing strength and warmth to build trust, connection and credibility

In Chapter 2 we looked at the style of leadership that is needed in our times – one that balances strength and warmth, relationships and results. This builds trust, connection and credibility.

I'm going to take you through four core behaviours that focus specifically on supporting you to balance warmth and strength:
- empathy
- active listening
- adopting a humble mindset
- assertive communication.

These core behaviours will ensure you show people you care, that you treat them with respect and speak with clarity and decisiveness, building connection, while emphasising your credibility and trustworthiness. Having power with, not over, others will cultivate relationships and get results.

As we address each behaviour, I will ask you some questions to reflect on where you sit with these today.

Empathy

Demonstrating empathy shows you care, which builds trust and connection.

Empathy is the ability to see the perspective of another – through their eyes – to be able to tune in and sense what they feel, and to express care for them. And to do this while maintaining your separateness and being objective.

Daniel Pink, author of *A Whole New Mind*, defines empathy as, 'the ability to imagine yourself in someone else's position and to intuit what that person is feeling. It is the ability to stand in others' shoes, to see with their

CHAPTER 5: LEADERSHIP PRESENCE

eyes, and to feel with their hearts'.

In your role as a leader, to achieve ongoing results with others, engaging and influencing them is essential. This is more challenging than ever given the varied nature of teams and how geographically dispersed they are. This calls for you to have the ability to meet the needs of a diverse range of people, to be other-focused and to take the time to understand their perspective. Without this, others will not feel seen nor heard and you will miss the opportunity to connect with and motivate your team, stakeholders and peers.

Leaders who demonstrate empathy
- take an interest in their co-workers' concerns
- actively demonstrate this in words, tone and action
- overtly communicate that they care.

Through this connection they are better able to intuit a co-worker's feelings or needs, and have a good sense of how they may see a particular situation.

Let's see what this looks like in action.

> My client 'Blake' explained he was feeling frustrated with his direct report – 'Charlie'. Charlie had not been offered the promotion she had been anticipating and had become reactionary and negative as a result. Her behaviour was impacting the team. It was for this very reason, her reactionary behaviour, that the management team had decided not to progress her to the next

management level. Blake set up a one on one meeting to give Charlie constructive feedback and support her growth and development. He wanted her to be ready the next time around. Blake took an empathic approach and, in our session, reflected on how this had supported a favourable outcome:

'When we met face to face, Charlie launched into her story and she was visibly upset and frustrated. I gave her the space to talk, instead of defending myself or the organisational decisions. I tuned in to how she was feeling. In the space of 10 minutes her body language relaxed as she spoke and I listened, and she saw that I understood. I didn't agree, but I understood. This completely changed the trajectory of our meeting.

Having connected on this level, I was then able to give her constructive feedback that would support her promotional aspirations moving forward, as well as ensure she was more focused on her behaviour with the team. She was able to hear this because I had started with empathy. That 10 minutes made all the difference. We both moved forward positively'.

The prerequisite for empathy is emotional self-awareness, starting with understanding the bodily sensations we feel before we tune into those of another. We covered this in Chapter 3.

When in meetings or interacting with others, ask yourself what another may be thinking or feeling in that moment. Be curious. Make a concerted effort to ask more questions. Pause. Be other-focused. By doing this in low stake situations, you can practise and prepare for more stressful times. When the stakes are higher, you are more likely to have to work harder to remain empathic.

Simple ways you can demonstrate empathy include:
- acknowledging a team member is stressed and suggesting they take a break
- offering greater flexibility to meet a family commitment
- providing development opportunities for an employee who is keen to progress.

It is important to recognise that as a leader you need to balance empathy with emotional regulation. A leader who is too empathetic may become overly embroiled in the needs or emotions of another, or be unable to provide constructive feedback when necessary. The key here is to empathise and appreciate the other's perspective, while remaining objective.

> **Reflection on empathy**
>
> - What helps you feel empathy?
>
> - Do you feel you are able to demonstrate and utilise empathy in all contexts?
>
> - When do you find it easier to feel empathic towards another? Clients tell me they feel more empathetic towards people they trust, respect or if they understand the situation another person is facing, perhaps due to a shared experience.
>
> - Are there certain people with whom you are less able to feel empathy towards? Perhaps where the person has shown you a lack of respect or interest?

Empathy is a skill you can learn. And it takes practise. As you reflect on the above questions, make a note of what resonates with you. Use the Leadership Presence Action Plan at the end of this chapter to guide you.

And one final point: practise does not mean you will get it right every time, but you always have the option to go back and repair. To say to someone, 'I don't think I managed our conversation very well. Can I try again?'

That takes empathic leadership.

Active listening

Active listening is vital for keeping the balance between relationships and results. When others do not feel heard by you, they are less likely to listen to you or feel safe enough to share their perspective. Building the capacity to actively listen establishes trust and connection. You may not agree with another's perspective, but by tuning in to them, you show you care. You cultivate the relationship.

At the same time, as you actively listen, you create space for others to share their ideas. This enables collaboration and collective problem solving. You promote results, through relationships.

I work with some clients who find it challenging to take the time to actively listen to others. There are a myriad of reasons for this, and they are not usually because my client is trying to be difficult or challenging, even though they are often perceived as such in these moments. Instead, they are passionate about the topic, or perhaps they disagree vehemently with the person speaking, or they are short on time and want to get to the solution they have prepared. Some have had an emotional reaction to something someone has said and were not able to self-regulate in the moment. Their intention is good; they want to get to a solution. In the process though, they become disconnected with their colleague(s) and the very solution they are trying to drive becomes difficult to execute. And the very people they need to support with their initiative are the same people they have not taken the time to connect with in previous interactions.

Active listening may feel counter-intuitive, especially when you are under pressure to get to an outcome and produce results, but if you are able to put your own opinions to one side and focus on the other person, you are more likely to create an opening for a real conversation – one in which you can both feel heard. This is the platform upon which you will co-create solutions and achieve buy-in.

Non-verbal communication

A key factor for developing your ability to actively listen is non-verbal communication. Keep in mind that much of what you communicate is conveyed through your body language. Pay attention to your tone, pace and body language, such as eye contact, to ensure your desire to actively listen is not being misconstrued. For instance, a client I worked with would lean towards the person he was talking with to show interest. However, he received feedback that through this action he was being perceived as aggressive. Be mindful of softening your stance and your eye contact, and consider whether it is appropriate to smile.

Your mindset is key to supporting your non-verbal

communication. By remaining curious and other-focused, and by adopting a position of respect, your overall interpersonal communication is likely to be aligned. As Sigmund Freud, an Austrian neurologist and the founder of psychoanalysis, noted, 'He that has eyes to see and ears to hear may convince himself that no mortal can keep a secret. If his lips are silent, he chatters with his fingertips; betrayal oozes out of him at every pore'. Here is an example.

> I recently worked with a client who had been advised by his manager and various peers that he was coming across as too direct and dogged in his drive towards results. To gain a more in-depth analysis to support my client's reflection and development, I conducted a series of 360-degree feedback sessions with various members of my client's team and peers, and with his manager.
>
> The feedback showed clear themes across all stakeholders. While my client was seen as extremely direct, this in itself was not seen as a negative. Many valued his willingness not to be afraid to disagree, and be brave and tough instead of toeing the line, as well as putting differing views on the table and offering diversity of thought. However, the negativity was created because, when interacting with his co-workers, he

was being perceived as being driven by achieving solutions at all costs. He was not keeping the relationship as a key focus.

I work with many clients who receive similar feedback. The overarching message from their peers is that they are knowledgeable and widely respected, but if they were able to adapt a more open approach, one in which they actively listened to their colleagues and created a relationship of mutual respect, they would be formidable.

My client reflected on his 360-degree feedback and made the conscious decision to adjust his style in the following ways when interacting with his co-workers:

- He spent more time asking others to share their perspective or specific challenges.

- He learnt to paraphrase what others had said to ensure they felt heard.

- He asked for feedback when sharing potential solutions and used open-ended questions, rather than making statements.

- He worked hard to avoid negative non-verbal communication such as folding his arms and

CHAPTER 5: LEADERSHIP PRESENCE

sighing when frustrated. Instead he smiled and used open gestures.

- He was mindful about topping and tailing emails with gentler and more engaging introductions and conclusions, rather than adopting a short, sharp tone. In other words, he avoided responding purely to the content of the email and reminded himself to interact with the addressee on a human level.

As he embedded these practices, my client shared, 'I am a results and action orientated person and I always want to keep things moving and get to a result as quickly as possible. I usually have a preconceived idea or opinion as I go into a meeting, but I now make the effort to hold it, initially. I can sometimes feel a little frustrated by this, as it is not my natural style. However, I can see the positive benefits of allowing the time to hear others' perspectives and consider their approach. It is clear that the more I do this, the more others are comfortable to share their ideas, and their approach. I have also noticed that this usually results in stronger buy-in of the final solution from my team and stakeholders'.

Overall, he reflected, 'I have come to realise that sometimes it is better to step back and review before I make a comment, to notice what is happening around me. I work hard to pause and ensure I don't overtake the conversation. I have learned to let people in, to focus on trust and create connection. I can see the positive impact this has had. I have generated more impactful relationships, which has supported us to collaborate and get to results more effectively'.

Reflection on active listening

Reflect on a recent conversation in which you felt actively listened to? What was the person doing to support you in feeling this way?

Interestingly, 'listen' and 'silent' may have the same letters, but active listening is much more powerful than just keeping quiet. Active listening requires you to listen and respond in a way that focuses on what the speaker is saying, and to be able to relate back to the speaker the content and feelings in the message to enhance understanding.

Take a moment to consider how effectively you utilise the following active listening techniques:

CHAPTER 5: LEADERSHIP PRESENCE

- Paraphrasing, which requires you to interpret in your own words what the speaker has said and repeat it back to them.

- Reflecting facts, checking your understanding of the content or factual aspect of what the speaker has said.

- Reflecting back feelings, as appropriate, and conveying empathy.

Summarise key themes you heard. Make a note of what stands out for you as areas to refine and work on as you develop your active listening skills. You can incorporate this into your Leadership Presence Action Plan.

Humble mindset

We saw in Chapter 2 that in these complex times leaders need to accept they are no longer the experts with all the solutions. This calls for humility and a willingness to give everyone, including yourself, the opportunity to explore, to learn, to practise and to fail.

This is an argument supported by Dan Cable, a professor of organisational behaviour at the London Business School. In his book *Alive at Work* he says that for leaders to adopt a humble mindset means having the 'humility, courage and insight to admit that they can benefit from the expertise of others who have less power than them'.

Of course, the buck stops with you as the leader, but if you don't train and flex these new leadership muscles, you risk missing out on a huge opportunity to gain from others' insights, as well as keep them engaged and productive.

As Dan Cable writes, 'Humble leaders help other people seek their potential, and experiment toward that potential. This is a gift that makes other people want to give back and want to follow'. So rather than seeing you as weak (a concern I hear from some when I suggest a humbler approach) your people see you as more confident, and they will feel more engaged along the way.

A leader I work with makes a point of saying to her leadership team, 'I don't know the answer here, can anyone help me?' She encourages her team to speak up, to suggest a solution and to do the same with each other. She speaks with confidence, and, through her words and actions, demonstrates that it is quite acceptable to find a solution together. She understands that so much is uncertain. She can't possibly have all the answers. She is modelling humble leadership. This generates an inclusive team and she gets to results quickly; the outcomes are co-created.

Making it a habit to ask questions and be curious

CHAPTER 5: LEADERSHIP PRESENCE

supports the modelling of a humble mindset. Rather than making you look uninformed this practice will foster motivation and engagement. This is an argument supported by Tim Westergren, co-founder of Pandora. He says in a Harvard Business Review video, 'I really do think that people are very, very motivated by leaders who they view as humble. I think it is an inspiring attribute. You want to work for someone who is like that, and more importantly, you model that for people who work for you. So, if you do that as a leader, you build humble leaders who then, in turn, build motivated teams'. This also builds the capacity of the team to make decisions and be more self-reliant, thereby reducing dependence on the leader.

You may choose to ask open and broad questions if you are looking to invite a wide selection of perspectives, for instance, 'Does anyone have anything to offer here?' Or perhaps you are looking for thoughts on a specific agenda item, such as, 'Can you make any suggestions on how to improve our virtual team meetings?' Overall, the key here is that you are explicitly letting the team know you value and expect their input.

You are welcoming an open conversation that supports relationships and trust. You are demonstrating a humble mindset.

Reflection on humble mindset

Take a moment to consider humble leadership. How well do you demonstrate this style of leadership?

- How comfortable are you with asking questions, and voicing that you would like to hear the perspectives of others?

- How could you actively model a humble leadership approach within your team and across your stakeholders? Do you know other leaders who do this well?

- Do you find yourself resisting the notion that you alone can't solve the problem, or are you open to co-creating solutions with others? Can you see the benefits of involving your team, stakeholders, peers and acting together on their suggestions?

As you reflect on these questions, make a note of what resonates for you. This can be incorporated into your Leadership Presence Action Plan.

CHAPTER 5: LEADERSHIP PRESENCE

Assertive communication

Empathy, humble mindset and active listening sit closer to the warmth end of the warmth/strength spectrum. We need to remember that strength also has a place. There are times when your team need you to be clear and decisive. For example, in the above section on active listening, I addressed the importance of hearing another's perspective. In this section, I am highlighting the necessity of being able to clearly articulate your views on the issue at hand while continuing to build trust and connection.

A practical example of this is when giving candid feedback. A high-performing team needs to be able to receive honest and open feedback. Assertive communication, aligned with the skills we have already addressed, is a critical component to this.

Assertive communication requires you to balance sharing your views and needs, while not restricting the other's ability to reply and share their perspective. You align this with appropriate body language, including good eye contact, a tone that is clear without being threatening or unapproachable, and an upright posture. You are firm, clear and respectful.

According to Sylvia Ann Hewlett, an economist and expert on gender and workplace issues, 'Real leaders listen, gather critical information, weigh the options carefully, look for a timely opening, and then demand action'. Such leaders are able to find the middle ground between passive and aggressive communication. This is assertiveness.

PASSIVE   ASSERTIVE   AGGRESSIVE

Being decisive and demanding action when appropriate requires good assertive communication skills. The key is in striking a balance.

Daniel Ames, a professor at Columbia Business School, and Francis Flynn, a professor at Stanford Graduate School of Business, conducted a number of studies in which they gathered employees' views of their colleagues' leadership strengths and weaknesses. They found that assertiveness was the problem most frequently raised, at times more so than intelligence, charisma and self-discipline combined.

Ames and Flynn's research showed that potential leaders tend to be at one end of the passive to aggressive scale or the other. In one study, they reviewed 1,000 comments made by co-workers. Overall, more than half of the descriptions of leadership weaknesses made clear references to assertiveness, with 48% suggesting too much assertiveness (at the aggressive end of the spectrum) and the remainder highlighting too little (at the passive end.)

Aggressive leaders can be toxic, closing off relationships and their ability to generate outcomes. They are focused on 'winning' or getting their point across and are not focused on the other person. This may be a useful tactic to generate fear and get results in the short term, but they will not instil trust and results over the long term. Behaviours associated with aggressive communication include shouting, giving ultimatums, using hurtful language, and non-verbal gestures such as pointing.

Conversely, a passive communicator will concede to another's demands and will not clearly deliver their message to another. Passive leaders are unlikely to be effective or achieve results. They will compromise and fail to pursue what they need to avoid conflict. Behaviours associated with passive communication include remaining silent or being overly polite.

Aggressive or passive communication styles can become problematic and both are non-assertive.

Assertive communication is relating to others in a clear, direct, open way without wielding power or applying undue pressure. It is respectful and keeps the focus on the building and the maintenance of relationships. Assertive communication ensures you are candid and credible, but not controlling. There is a distinct difference, and a vital one if you hope to build trust and connection when leading others.

As a leader you will always need to navigate your way productively through conversations and conflict. Let's look at a hypothetical scenario and see how to do this with assertive communication.

Imagine one of your team members, 'John', has committed to getting a report to you by 4pm, in time for you to incorporate it into a final document to share with the board the following day. It is now 5.30pm and, when you go to look for John, you realise he has left the office and you are unable to reach him. You work into the evening, generating the necessary information to complete your document for the board.

Given your likely levels of frustration, it is possible when seeing John the next day, you may take an aggressive stance, calling him into your office, raising your voice to get your message across that you never want that to happen again. Alternatively, you could take a more passive position, and not address the issue at all with John.

Or you could embrace assertive communication and share the impact the situation had on you and your desired expectations for the future.

To support you with this I have created the following acronym:

Raise the issue, and express the

Impact on you (state your issue without blaming anyone. Do not label the other person, e.g. 'You are lazy'), then explain your

Desired expectation for the future.

An example of how to apply this could be:

R: 'John, I asked you to get that report to me by 4pm yesterday'.

I: 'When I discovered you'd left for the evening and had failed to send me the information, I felt frustrated and let down'.

D: 'Next time, if I give you a deadline, I'd like you to let me know if you foresee an issue. And let me know if you are going to miss it'.

I encourage you to finish this statement with, 'Is there anything you need from me to make this happen?' This ensures the accountability remains with your co-worker while demonstrating your level of support.

For example, John may not have sent the report to you because he did not have the skills to generate the necessary data. He may be more inclined towards a passive style of communication. Without this final statement, you are not opening up the option for John to reply to your request, and to take the necessary steps to upskill, and support you better in the long run. This simple final statement will allow you to build trust and connection, and ensure a better outcome in the future.

Reflection on assertive communication

- As you review the passive – assertive – aggressive spectrum, where do you currently sit?

- Does this change depending on the context – for instance, if you are in a high stake situation or close to a deadline?

- Do you find it harder to be assertive with certain types of people – for instance, a person with a particular style or position of power?

- Do you effectively step back and listen? Or do you go into meetings with a preconceived idea? Are you able to pause before jumping in with a comment?

- Do you feel you are able to speak up in a meeting for an idea you feel strongly about? Does this vary depending on who is in the meeting?

- Think of a recent occasion when you wanted to let someone else know that you were unhappy or dissatisfied with a result they produced. Did you find it challenging to give them this feedback? Is it harder to speak up with one person, and less so with another?

As a leader, to remain focused on both relationships and results, it is important you are able to use assertive communication to share honest and robust feedback. Having the ability to speak up candidly while also demonstrating respect and care for the other person is an ideal way to build connection, while not losing sight of results. As you reflect on the above questions, consider what you would like to incorporate into your Leadership Presence Action Plan.

Reading the context

Bringing your genuine self to your role of leadership comes with a caveat. And that caveat is context.

The elements that define a good leader in one context may not work in another, and ideal leadership behaviours may vary across organisations. For example, what is required in a large financial institution may be very different to what is required in a small family run business, or a large government agency. Likewise, what is required in your role as a leader may be different to what is required in your role of parent or friend. You are still you, but you may need to adjust based on the context.

In your role of leader, while it is important to remain genuine, you may need to modify your behaviour to fit with the environment or particular needs of the situation at hand.

For instance, one of your key strengths may be your detail orientation – your ability to absorb, contribute and get across a lot of information. If you are working on a complex report with your team, diving into the detail with them may be imperative. However, if you are presenting a strategic overview to the board, you will need to lift out of that detail.

Likewise, if a part of your genuine self is to use a lot of humour, to find the funny side of things or be flippant, this will not be appropriate in various work contexts. You may find that you need to 'dial up' or 'down' depending on the situation at hand. If you are about to share some bad news with the team, humour is unlikely to be appropriate. Yet, when giving a celebratory speech about a colleague, humour is probably welcomed.

With each of these examples, you may know this instinctively but lose sight when under pressure, or when feeling tired or frustrated.

To demonstrate Leadership Presence, it is important to be clear how to modify your behaviour, or dial up or down, as required.

I am not suggesting that you compromise or 'sell out' to the extent you no longer feel genuine. In fact, I have worked with executives over the years who have felt their personal values were misaligned with the culture of their organisation to such an extent that they have made the decision to move on. By doing their Inner Presence work, they became clear on their non-negotiables.

CHAPTER 5: LEADERSHIP PRESENCE

Being mindful of nuanced contextual considerations and adjusting your style and approach to fit organisational and situational contexts is essential in demonstrating Leadership Presence.

Leadership Presence at a glance

In Chapter 2 I encouraged you to focus on relationships to get to results. The behaviours outlined above will help you build trust and connection with others to cultivate those relationships.

I've also said leadership is contextual, and so it is important to decide the type of leader you want to be, and to understand how you are being perceived by others. Now we are going to create your Leadership Presence learning and development plan to help you gain clarity on this and generate an action plan to bridge any gaps between the two.

This will help you to build a list of key themes to work on to ensure you are exhibiting the leadership behaviours needed to demonstrate Leadership Presence.

Leadership Presence learning and development plan

A key to Leadership Presence is being intentional about how you want to be perceived by others in each and every context, and being clear about the behaviour you want to exhibit and model.

To support my clients to get to this point we work through a series of exercises. Everyone comes in with a different set of skills and issues, so I tailor reflective exercises and actions to their particular situation. There is no one-size-fits-all solution.

I don't know your starting point, so I can't tailor exercises for you, but I can step you through a process to decide the type of leader you want to be and discover how close you are to the mark, in the eyes of both yourself and others. This will help you understand what areas to work on. I'll give you some examples of common themes that arise for my clients, as some may resonate with you.

I have provided you with a Leadership Presence Action Plan template to capture your findings. It is then over to you to be your own coach. Remember, we are continually learning and adapting, so go easy on yourself. Take it step by step. The key is to be, and remain, intentional. It is about being the leader you want and chose to be – for yourself and for others.

CHAPTER 5: LEADERSHIP PRESENCE

There are three steps:
1. Decide the type of leader you want to be.
2. Discover how you are perceived now.
3. Develop your Leadership Presence Action Plan.

Let's get started.

Step 1. Decide type of leader you want to be

Start by reviewing the leadership behaviours I have outlined in this chapter (empathy, active listening, humble mindset and assertive communication). Having reviewed the reflective questions, in each section, what resonated? What would you like to refine? Use the Leadership Presence Action Plan at the end of this chapter to guide you.

How do you want to be viewed as a leader? How would you like others to describe you? Consider the following questions to support your reflection:

- Think of a leader you are inspired by. This can be someone you know, worked for or with, or someone famous, past or present. What behaviours did they exhibit that you admire? What did they do that made you want to follow them and enjoy working with them?

- Now consider a leader you didn't enjoy working with. What behaviours did they exhibit that you didn't like, or found ineffective?

- Think back to a day or time you got home and thought, 'I did a really good job today'. How were you acting on that day? What stands out for you?

Reflect on your responses to the above questions and write a list of clear bullet points on the type of leader you want to be.

Now answer the question: *What is my leadership style when I'm leading as my best self?* Refer to your SWOT analysis from Chapter 4 as you consider this question.

Now distil this:
- What three words would you use to describe your leadership style?
  - If you're struggling, what words would your manager use? If you don't know, have a guess.
  - What words would your direct reports use, or other stakeholders?
  - What words would you like them to be saying?

- Now come up with three words to describe your leadership style, and complete the sentence.
  I am _____, _____, and _____.

When I ask my clients to do this, they struggle to come up with three words initially. However, as they start to reflect on and describe their leadership style, who they

CHAPTER 5: LEADERSHIP PRESENCE

are aspiring to be as a leader and who they have been when they are at their best, their body language clearly shows they feel empowered. They are energised by this process.

Here are some examples from my clients:
- I am a credible, empathetic and accountable leader.
- I am an empathetic, strong and professional leader.
- I am a decisive, genuine and caring leader.

This is an outward demonstration of your Inner Presence and ensures congruence between how you act and who you are.

Step 2. Discover how you are perceived

As Leadership Presence is largely about perception rather than concrete facts, collect feedback from people around you.

When working with clients to develop their Leadership Presence, I conduct 30-minute interviews with their key stakeholders, managers, peers and direct reports. Feedback varies of course, yet there tends to be consistent themes that come through the conversations. This provides my client with clear areas to work on, and real-life examples from which to build a Leadership Presence development and coaching plan.

Examples of feedback I might receive:
- X is warm and approachable.

- X offers a diverse perspective.
- X is outcomes-focused, dogged and resilient.
- X needs to devote more time to strategic imperatives and be less involved in the details.
- X should build stronger engagement with cross-functional teams.
- X needs to utilise more of an active listening approach.

While it may be uncomfortable, there is no reason why you can't do this for yourself.

Select a handful of people who have seen you interact in various situations, day-to-day and in high stake situations. This may be your manager, one peer and two direct reports. Pick people you trust and respect, and people you feel will be able to give you honest and direct feedback and won't just be nice to you.

Ensure the person is aware that you will not hold their feedback against them and that you value their perspective. Be clear that you are collating feedback to understand key themes you can work on.

Here are the types of questions I ask, which you can use or customise to fit your own needs:
- What do you see as my strengths? (This can be useful to start as it's a broad question.)
- What do you see as my development opportunities?
- What would you like to see me doing more of?
- What would you like to see me doing less of?

CHAPTER 5: LEADERSHIP PRESENCE

- What would you like to see me stop doing, start doing or keep doing?

Remember, the goal is to understand key themes to work on. It is useful to ask for specific examples of times you've demonstrated a particular behaviour being discussed. This gives you tangible examples to reflect on. On the other hand, try not to get overly caught in the detail.

You may find you want to defend yourself when you hear the feedback, or you may feel uncomfortable. Work hard to remain curious and listen. Remind yourself that while the feedback is useful, it is subjective. And it is incredibly useful – this is your opportunity for growth.

Be relaxed. If you look uncomfortable or upset, the other person will recognise this and start to minimise their sharing. Always remember to thank the person for being generous and courageous enough to provide you with feedback. Remember, it is quite possible this was uncomfortable for them too.

The feedback provided gives you clear data on how you are perceived by others. Review the data to draw out key themes – both strengths and areas for development.

Step 3. Develop your Leadership Presence Action Plan

You now have three sources of information to draw from:

- your self-reflection on your leadership style
- your reflection on leadership behaviours that build trust and connection
- the key themes you've drawn out from the feedback you've collected.

The next step is to compare your self-reflection alongside the perception of others. What are the key themes that emerge? Where are the most significant gaps, and strongest alignment?

Pay attention to any areas where your perception is quite different from the feedback you have received. This indicates potential blind spots to work on. By closing these gaps you can feel confident you are being seen by others in the way you intended.

As you review, consider areas that will have the most impact and create the biggest wins for you. This is very individual, so I encourage you to take your time with this exercise.

Let me give you an example.

I have gathered feedback on behalf of clients whose stakeholders have stated they are 'too blunt and direct'. Some clients, when hearing this feedback, aren't shocked, knowing they have a particularly direct communication style. The feedback, however, reinforces their need to

CHAPTER 5: LEADERSHIP PRESENCE

refine their style (as they are getting their stakeholders off-side, and this is starting to damage relationships and their career prospects).

However, other clients have not expected their 360-degree feedback group to perceive them as 'too direct and blunt'. This comes as a surprise. As we reflect on why they have received such feedback, some come to realise it is borne out of frustration, perhaps because they have recently missed out on a work opportunity and feel demotivated, or because they do not have sufficient organisational resources to get their job done and have become solely task focused. In this instance, we work to resolve the underlying issue.

I share this example to illustrate the importance of taking your time to reflect not only on the themes that emerge, but also addressing any underlying cause.

What actions do you need to take to address your findings? Add these to your Leadership Presence Action Plan.

Following are some common themes (not an exhaustive list) that emerge when conducting a 360-degree feedback review for my clients. You may choose to reflect on these as you consider where you want to be, and where you are today.

Common strengths:
- depth and breadth of knowledge
- people focused

- enterprise mindset
- able to offer a diverse perspective
- provides candid feedback
- strong work ethic
- results driven
- creates a loyal team
- provides a broad and diverse perspective
- passionate about chosen field
- ability to work across multiple priorities.

Common development areas:
- interpersonal communication – increase awareness of impact on others
- give greater focus on securing buy-in from others
- manage frustration – ensure this doesn't show up in interactions with others
- lift out of the detail – consider broader context
- empower team – let go of detail
- strategic focus – create more time for this
- focus on wider consultation with business
- target appropriate level of detail for various audiences.

Now it is time to finalise the areas you would like to start working on. Use the following Leadership Presence Action Plan to guide you.

CHAPTER 5: LEADERSHIP PRESENCE

LEADERSHIP PRESENCE ACTION PLAN: BRINGING IT ALL TOGETHER

Your leadership style

(Refer to 'Decide type of leader you want to be' section above). Remember, this is the leader you would like to be consistently, leading as your 'best self'.

I am _____ , _____ ,

and _____ .

Leadership behaviours that build trust and connection

What resonated as you reviewed the reflective questions under each leadership behaviour covered in this chapter? What would you like to focus on and refine to develop your Leadership Presence?

Empathy _____

Active listening _____

Humble mindset _____

Assertive communication _____

_____

Key themes to emerge from 360-degree feedback process

Strengths

_____

_____

_____

_____

_____

_____

Development areas

_____

_____

_____

_____

_____

_____

CHAPTER 5: LEADERSHIP PRESENCE

Areas to work on (examples provided below)

Key area of focus _____

Strength or development area _____

Action steps

_____

_____

Desired outcome

_____

_____

Impact on my Leadership Presence

_____

_____

_____

Example 1.
Key area of focus: Provide context
Strength or development area: Development area

Action steps:
When making requests, start by explaining the rationale and provide background information. Give others the WHY.

Desired outcome: Secure buy-in.

Impact on my Leadership Presence:
My team will be clearer about why I am asking for their input on project X, and why I am asking them to work to a tight deadline. They will feel more motivated as they are clear on how this ties back to broader context.

Example 2.
Key area of focus: Assertive communication
Strength or development area: Strength

Action steps:
Continue to keep a focus on providing 'in the moment' feedback with my direct reports (balance this with empathy).

CHAPTER 5: LEADERSHIP PRESENCE

> **Desired outcome:**
> Mutual accountability to ensure Project X gets completed on time.
>
> **Impact on my Leadership Presence:**
> My team will get more comfortable with speaking up, sharing feedback to ensure we keep driving outcomes together. They will also know I care about their development – and this will support trust and connection within the team.

What's next?

In Chapter 6, we look at Team Presence – how to produce results with others, by navigating team dynamics, adopting intentional communication and learning to foster a team environment that embraces collective learning and problem solving. A team that produces effective and innovative results together.

CHAPTER 6

TEAM PRESENCE

The responsibility of leadership is not to come up with all the ideas but to create an environment in which great ideas can happen.

SIMON SINEK
START WITH WHY

Inner Presence and Leadership Presence are two legs of a three-legged stool. Without the third leg, Team Presence, you won't achieve effective results *collectively*.

And it is *with others* that you will be most effective, especially in these complex times – with others, in teams.

Your team members are involved in interdependent, knowledge-based work – which involves individuals working with others, in teams, and more than one team working together. (Do you remember the last time you completed an entire project on your own?) To be successful means having to ask questions, use cognition, and work with constant change, remaining in ongoing communication, and sharing issues and concerns. To get the best from people, you will need to create an environment where people can do their best work. This is where Team Presence comes in.

Developing Team Presence requires you to be aware of your behaviours, actions and the voice you bring to team settings as well as the voice you allow in others, so they can do the same. You have done the groundwork for this in previous chapters. Now you are ready to bring your skills and awareness to this final, essential domain of presence.

I define Team Presence as: *Cultivating an environment that empowers teams to collaborate, learn and innovate.*

For the purpose of this book, I'm using the term 'team' to encompass your involvement in any group you work with to produce results. Whether it's a team of three or ten, a team of peers or a team you manage, the key focus is that you are achieving results *together*.

Team Presence encapsulates:
- fostering psychological safety
- using intentional communication
- understanding team dynamics.

CHAPTER 6: TEAM PRESENCE

Psychological safety

Psychological safety, as defined by Amy Edmondson, the Novartis Professor of Leadership at Harvard Business School, in her book *The Fearless Organization,* is 'a climate in which people are comfortable expressing and being themselves'. Psychological safety is not the only element needed for teams to succeed, but it *is* the most important. It is the gateway to high performing teams.

If a workplace is low in psychological safety, people will be reluctant to share what they know. They'll be fearful of being wrong, being shown as incompetent, negative or unhelpful, or that they might offend someone, especially you, their boss. Instead of just focusing on the job at hand, people tend to also focus on looking good, or not looking inadequate. In other words, they don't play to win, they play to avoid losing.

By contrast, in a workplace that is high in psychological safety, people will feel safe and valued for openly sharing what they think or know, even if it's only a concern, a half-formed idea, a question, or that they've made a mistake. By sharing, others can then build on their contributions and they can all learn together.

In organisations where people have worked to create psychological safety, they've explicitly declared they want to create a place where people want to come to work, a place where people are comfortable to jump right in and feel able to talk openly about the work they are doing. The results are twofold: these workplaces are creating more productive, innovative teams and, thus, are finding a competitive edge.

This is supported by a two-year study conducted at Google, named Project Aristotle, designed to understand what makes a team effective within their organisation. The research, involving 15,000 employees, discovered the most important aspect was that team members felt safe to take risks and be vulnerable in front of each other. Their research showed their gateway to team effectiveness was *psychological safety*.

Psychological safety is still not common practice and there is a simple reason for this. Fear. Fear of 'looking bad'. In the absence of a psychologically safe environment, we hold back. We wait. We seek more information. We walk past things. It is better not to upset someone, we tell ourselves, or look incapable, obstructive or uninformed.

The concept of psychological safety may sound simple. It is not. It takes intentional communication.

Teams that are low in psychological safety, are at higher risk of preventable business failures because workers are fearful of retribution.

Let's consider an example. By the end of the 1990s Korean Air had one of the world's worst safety records in the industry. In the previous 20 years the airline had a series of accidents that resulted in over 700 fatalities. Malcolm Gladwell, journalist and author, discusses

CHAPTER 6: TEAM PRESENCE

these events in his book *Outliers: The Story of Success*.

Gladwell argued that the issue wasn't the quality of the planes or the training of the pilots, it was the entrenched cultural values of respecting authority. While safety depends on pilots and co-pilots working together as a team, co-pilots at Korean Air respected authority greatly. They didn't feel safe enough to go against their more senior pilots, even in dire circumstances.

Once Korean Air realised that their problem was cultural, they addressed it by creating a new training program for their pilots, encouraging them to speak up about potential danger, admit mistakes and not to be overly polite or vague in their language.

This is a powerful example of the value of creating a culture of psychological safety. It also highlights that psychological safety goes hand in hand with high performance. Allowing the co-pilots to speak openly and admit mistakes in no way reduced their responsibility.

High performance in a psychologically safe workplace

Amy Edmondson, author of *The Fearless Organization*, makes the distinction between *psychological safety* and *performance standards*. Both are necessary when it comes to creating high performing teams.

A psychologically safe environment does not mean losing focus on performance or refraining from holding people to account. However, without psychological safety, no matter how hard you push or try to empower your team to achieve results, they are always going to hold back. It's like trying to drive fast with the handbrake on.

Edmondson expands further by drawing out four potential zones a team may find themselves in, depending on the level of focus they give to each of these two dimensions – *psychological safety* and *performance standards*. The four zones are:

1. apathy zone
2. anxiety zone
3. comfort zone
4. high performance zone.

In a situation where the leader is pushing hard for results but has not created sufficient psychological safety, the team is likely to be in the anxiety zone. Conversely, an environment high in psychological safety but one in which the team is not being motivated to produce results is likely to be sitting in the comfort zone. A team that doesn't have a focus on either psychological safety or performance standards is likely to find themselves in the apathy zone.

The high performance zone is one in which the leader, and their team, has created the conditions for high psychological safety while also striving for high performance and results. This is a team that is likely to be performing to a high standard, while learning and innovating.

You may be concerned that if you allow your team to talk about 'unformed ideas', it could open a can of

CHAPTER 6: TEAM PRESENCE

worms. Perhaps people won't stop talking! Yet reducing fear and creating the right dialogue to generate new ideas and opportunities to learn should not be confused with getting the job done and holding people to account. This takes leadership.

Psychological safety is not about being nice or avoiding tough conversations. While I want you to liberate your team to speak up, I encourage you not to shy away from providing open, honest and constructive feedback. In fact, in a psychologically safe environment, it is much more likely that these types of conversations will occur.

I encourage you to set clear expectations for the team and to have the courage to provide necessary feedback, while demonstrating empathy. Brené Brown shares the phrase, 'Clear is kind. Unclear is unkind' in her book *Dare to Lead* and argues that, 'most of us avoid clarity because we tell ourselves that we're being kind, when what we're actually doing is being unkind and unfair'. Kim Scott, author of *Radical Candor*, offers a framework by the same name, in which she encourages leaders to 'care personally and challenge directly'.

What both Brown and Scott are talking about here is communication. Highly refined communication skills are key to fostering psychological safety and accountable teams.

Intentional communication

Intentional communication is considered and purposeful. It requires you to be able to speak up and actively listen, to voice your perspective while also taking the time to hear others. It asks you to keep relationships at the core and to be clear you are promoting the conditions for a positive group dynamic. This type of communication supports enhanced collaboration and ensures you navigate together, in partnership, towards more impactful outcomes.

Recently, I ran a session for a leadership team designed as part of a larger program to enhance team effectiveness. I spoke with each member of the team prior to the program to hear their challenges, opportunities and expectations. I also asked for permission to set the room up differently during their team sessions, saying, 'Can we avoid the use of desks and PowerPoint slides? Instead, can we sit in a circle, talk, share ideas and come up with solutions together?' I wanted to set myself up as the facilitator of the team's growth and learning, as opposed to the expert, and to support them in talking openly together, sharing ideas, gaining insight and awareness, and finding productive and implementable solutions.

We set up the room without desks, for the team session, to remove any barriers to communication. This is not commonplace in our corporate world. We are normally behind a desk, a laptop or a notepad. Initially,

CHAPTER 6: TEAM PRESENCE

there was reticence. I saw it in each team member's body language as they entered the room and took their seats. Their arms were crossed, and they appeared hesitant.

I started with the check-in process, inviting each person to share what was on their mind, as we begun. This process supported everyone to bring their voices into the room, to hear from one another, and allowed them to settle into the session. As the team went through the morning, sharing their challenges, struggles and insights with each other, as well as generating a plan and next steps, it was clear by their body language and how they communicated that they had visibly relaxed with each other. Their postures changed, they unfolded their arms and smiled more, used greater eye contact and lent towards each other.

As we checked out of the session (using the same process as the check-in), the team shared how they felt more connected and had seen each other in a new light. They committed to reaching out on a more regular basis. They had experienced each other on a human level, and this had a direct impact on their quality of communication and relationships.

This illustrates Amy Edmondson's argument in *The Fearless Organization* that team members are much more likely to openly share important information and insights and questions, 'where leaders have created conditions to make listening and speaking up the norm, not the exception'.

This is the heart of intentional communication.

Advocacy vs inquiry

Communicating with intent means you are capturing collective intelligence and moving away from fixed positions and pushing your own agenda.

Often, leaders (and their teams) take a position, fight for their perspective. Rather than actively participating in the discussion, they wait for their turn to speak then offer their pre-formulated position or perspective. As the stakes increase, they become more fixed in their view. Open communication has ceased.

By contrast, speaking up with your views while demonstrating you remain open to others' input keeps conversations moving productively. This challenging balancing act is described as 'advocacy and inquiry' by Professors Chris Argyris and Donald Schön, authors of *Organizational Learning II: Theory, method and practice*.

Advocacy is about challenging others' views without offending or alienating people – speaking up in a non-combative way. Doing this successfully means others are comfortable to share their thoughts in response to your ideas. They feel psychologically safe to participate in the discussion.

Inquiry is the art of being able to let go of your certainty, suspending your judgement, and listening respectfully to the other.

The art of navigating the turning point between

CHAPTER 6: TEAM PRESENCE

advocacy and inquiry is to recognise what William Isaacs refers to as *choice point* in his book *Dialogue: The Art of Thinking Together*. This is the point in the conversation where you choose to *defend* your argument rather than *suspend* your thinking. In Chapter 3, I talked about the importance of having the level of self-awareness needed to make a deliberate choice about how to respond versus how you react. This is one of those times. In conversation you can choose to defend your point of view (tighten your grip) or to suspend your perspective and try to understand another's point of view (loosen your grip).

As one of my coaching clients shared:

> 'I realised it is better for the team if I stopped trying to solve everyone's problems. It has made a change in the way I think. I'm pausing when I realise that I've started to tell others what I think rather than listening. I feel much more positive as a result. It is better for everyone'. He went on to explain, 'The other day, we had an incident at work. A team member suggested we sit together and debrief. I let them speak and we discussed what they had learned, and they came up with an improved way to manage a similar situation in the future. As the debrief drew to a conclusion, they noted I had talked a lot less than I usually do. I told them: I don't need to. Your suggestions are great'.

This is a great example of a leader suspending their thinking and allowing others in the team to speak up, share their views and be mutually accountable. This requires a shift in mindset for leaders who are more used to pushing their goals and ideas forward and, instead, asking what's your perspective here? What suggestions do you have? What are you thinking?

As always, context plays a role. Suspending your thinking is not *always* the answer. There are exceptions, such as if you are not looking to generate new ideas, or you need to make unilateral decisions and do not want rebuttal or inquiry. Or if you are unable to reveal your thinking in an emergency situation where you need people to move quickly, i.e. there's a fire in the building.

The key is to be clear that you have a choice to suspend or defend in every conversation.

Many of my coaching clients are fatigued with trying to push their solutions forward. The sense of relief is palpable when they shift their mindset to focus on their team, to work *with* them to find solutions.

SAIL framework

The concepts I discuss here are based on the work of William Isaacs, author of *Dialogue: The Art of Thinking Together*. Grounded in the work of Isaacs, I have created my SAIL framework to support you in balancing advocacy and inquiry and, more broadly, for having quality conversations with others.

CHAPTER 6: TEAM PRESENCE

The SAIL acronym:

Speaking is about speaking up and bringing your voice into the room.

Appreciation is about respecting others and appreciating that they may have different perspectives to yours which are just as valid.

Intermission is about pausing and suspending your beliefs – taking a brief intermission from your firmly held point of view.

Listening is about actively listening.

A yacht is propelled by its sail. By utilising the wind, a crew can propel themselves forward. Likewise, by swinging the boom around, they can use the wind to bring the boat to a dead stop.

This is a useful metaphor to reflect on the quality of your conversations. By using the various elements in the SAIL framework as you communicate, you are able to navigate through a conversation productively.

Let's review this:
- To *advocate* is to use speaking and appreciation.
- To *inquire* is to use listening and intermission.

If you are challenging a point of view or have an idea of your own that you want to voice, *speak up* and put it forward while remembering to *appreciate* the others' perspective. At the same time, it may be appropriate to have an *intermission* from your own perspective as you speak up, so that you can *listen* with open curiosity.

Navigating through all four of these elements (SAIL) will enable you to have a productive conversation. Different contexts will call for a different focus.

Linking back to psychological safety, as a leader you are encouraging your people to *speak*. This may not be comfortable for some and you will need to use *listen* and *intermission* in order to give others the space to *speak* and *appreciate*. This applies to your team members too. Generating a psychologically safe environment is a collective endeavour.

In our workplaces and in our teams, there is tension between advocacy and inquiry. The key is to be able to identify when to adopt each. You may find yourself resorting to advocacy as you focus on finding a solution, and quickly. If you do not balance this with genuine inquiry, talk has failed you and you will no longer be in dialogue. If in doubt, refer to SAIL. This framework is designed to support you to navigate conversations effectively.

> A client I worked with felt uncomfortable opposing an initiative put forward by her manager and peer group. She was performing an acting role and was particularly concerned about alienating her colleagues with her opposition, especially as they were in the process of deciding whether to make her role a permanent one.
>
> By using the SAIL framework to strike a balance, she was able to constructively challenge the initiative and voice her concerns. As she addressed this issue with the group, she chose to let them speak first, seeking to understand their perspective, while also taking an intermission from her own position. At the same time, she remained committed to speaking up with her thoughts and misgivings. As a result, she was delighted she had been able to voice what was important to her, and that the team were able to hear her perspective without defensiveness or concern.

> As she relayed this to me she said, 'I've learned to open up to adversity. I'm no longer fearful if my managers or peers don't agree with something I say or do'. She had given herself permission to speak up, knowing that she could do it in an appreciative way while demonstrating she had the best interests of her team and her organisation at heart.
>
> She elaborated, 'I accept that in my career and personal life, things will get uncomfortable at times, but that is when I grow and learn. Good sailors aren't made by only sailing on calm seas'.

I'm constantly astounded by my clients. It was such a privilege to witness her growth. This metaphor formed the basis of my SAIL framework!

Team dynamics

In today's working landscape you are likely to be a member of multiple teams. And the membership of these teams is likely to change regularly. As you move between teams, you will need to be able to adjust to each unique team dynamic.

A useful model for developing insight into your interpersonal communication patterns and those of your

CHAPTER 6: TEAM PRESENCE

team is the Four Player Model. You can use this in conjunction with the SAIL framework to 'read' and enable the quality of interactions in your team to work towards fostering psychological safety.

The Four Player Model was developed by David Kantor, an American psychologist, organisational consultant and clinical researcher. He has founded three research and training institutes, written numerous books and articles, and is the inventor of a series of psychometric instruments that provide insight into individual and group behaviours.

Kantor started out by studying families, recognising distinct patterns in the way they communicate, before applying his findings in the corporate world. He created the Four Player Model to provide a framework and language for leaders and their teams to understand and openly discuss their patterns of communication in a non-blaming and neutral way. According to Kantor, there isn't a good or a bad way of communicating. Instead, there are stuck patterns that emerge in teams, limiting conversational flow amongst its members.

If you and your colleagues are aware of these patterns and work to shift them, a new way of communicating opens up within the group. As Kantor argues, 'There is a direct correlation between the effectiveness of the team and the quality of their conversations'.

The Four Player Model looks at everything said by you and your teammates through four 'speech acts'.

These are:

1. Move – suggesting a way forward. This can be a direction, idea or task.

2. Follow – supporting someone else's suggestion or moving it to completion. This gives oxygen to the move. For instance, a follow would keep an idea on the table for further discussion.

3. Oppose – coming up with a counter argument, challenging or voicing a correction.

4. Bystand – actively reflecting on what is happening with the team members around us. Giving perspective, remaining neutral. This is important to help the team notice what's going on.

Kantor argues that at any point we are making one of these speech acts.

All speech acts are required

In every team, there needs to be someone willing to make a *move* to initiate an idea or a position. And for this idea to take effect, there needs to be another (or others) in the team willing to support this team member's move, as well as take the necessary action to see this through to completion (*follow*).

Others need to be willing to bring a counter argument (*oppose*). This allows for ideas to be corrected and refined. And finally, there needs to be team members willing or able to bring a neutral perspective to observe what they're seeing and share that openly (*bystand*).

CHAPTER 6: TEAM PRESENCE

It's important to keep in mind that, while this sounds straightforward, teams are often out of balance. People tend to take on specific roles and get stuck in them. For instance, they may always follow the leader, or they may always oppose a particular team member's perspective.

I witness leaders who are unintentionally stuck in patterns. Often, they are trying to drive a result and are focused on the outcome. With that goal in mind they are making consistent moves or opposing certain viewpoints or challenging the status quo, and they're advocating for a particular position with little inquiry. Lack of inquiry has the potential to create disengaged followers.

It won't work to oppose, or use any of the four speech acts, without considering the quality of that interaction. To support you with this, I encourage you to integrate the SAIL framework. This will enhance your ability to advocate and inquire effectively. As the captain of your ship, in order to sail your boat with clarity, it is important to **speak** up, actively **listen** and **appreciate** the other person's perspective while ensuring you take an **intermission** from your own view as necessary. This framework will ensure you approach the Four Player Model speech acts with the right mindset.

Have you worked in a team:
- with all movers and no followers?
- that didn't challenge or oppose in any way?

- that said they would follow but then didn't take action?
- in which opposers weren't accepted by the group?
- where two team members were stuck in a particular pattern, i.e., move-oppose-move-oppose?

These are examples of ineffective teams. The Four Player Model is another tool to add to your leadership toolkit. A way to get 'unstuck' and reflect on unhelpful communication patterns and navigate unchartered waters.

Understanding the Four Player Model and using the SAIL framework will help you create an environment where people can talk and think together, where you can galvanise teams and the connections between them, where you can interact with the team dynamics. This is your Team Presence in action.

Releasing the potential of teams

The world of work today is more geographically dispersed than ever before. There is no doubt that teams play a significant role in producing results in our complex world. Our engagement levels, our productivity, our creativity and our future organisational competitiveness and success are all intrinsically linked with how effectively we are able to produce outcomes, with others, within teams. Your people are part of the solution.

In the introduction of this book I asked you to imagine working with a team that is open, curious and safe enough to talk and think through problems together.

This is what you've been working towards.

CHAPTER 6: TEAM PRESENCE

By bringing your best self to your role of leader, refining your communication skills and fostering a positive team dynamic, you build trust and create connections between team members and across teams, allowing collaboration and collective intelligence to emerge. You have released the potential of your team.

Team Presence at a glance

As the leader, if you are displaying signals that you have all the answers and most valuable ideas, you will stop others from sharing theirs.

The SAIL framework combined with the Four Player Model provides you with a toolkit for intentional communication, equipping you to foster a psychologically safe environment. You're now equipped to speak up and move conversations forward productively; supporting others to do the same, whilst not losing sight of high performance. These go hand in hand.

The goal of Team Presence is to cultivate collaborative, innovative and accountable teams by supporting others to talk, think, learn and create together.

Go ahead and create the new benchmark. This is Team Presence.

Team Presence learning and development plan

Each client I work with has a different set of skills to work on to develop and refine their Team Presence. There isn't a standard solution that fits for everyone. Instead, I will walk you through a series of reflective exercises so you can get clear on the areas you would like to develop. I have provided you with an Action Plan template to complete so you can become your own coach. Completing the plan will hold you to account. Be intentional. If you are not accountable to yourself, how can you ask others to be accountable to you.

There are three steps:
1. Encapsulate learnings from previous chapters.
2. Reflect on your intentional communication skills.
3. Create your action plan and develop key skills.

Step 1. Encapsulate learnings from previous chapters

Chapter 3 – Emotional self-awareness and regulation and connecting to self
Continue to develop this capacity. Keep in mind, inconsistent behaviour can have an adverse effect.

Chapter 4 – Inner Presence
Ensure you are empowering yourself to be your best

self and remain authentic. This will support your team in feeling comfortable to do the same, to let their own masks down and be authentic. When people feel seen and accepted, they feel more connected.

Chapter 5 – Leadership Presence
- Use empathy and active listening skills. This will support others in feeling comfortable to speak up and will build the necessary connection for others to know you have their backs.

- Adopt a humble mindset as needed to support others in feeling comfortable to admit errors, challenge the status quo and ask more questions. This starts with you admitting your own mistakes. Normalise this for others.

- Use assertive communication to ensure you and others create a group norm that it is ok to give candid feedback. This ensures clear accountability. It will also support you in offering and inviting constructive feedback. Remember, psychological safety is not about being 'nice'. Set clear goals and engage in respectful dialogue to achieve them.

- Encourage others to adopt the 360-degree feedback process covered in Chapter 5. This will support the team to manage how they are being perceived by others and will help them view work as a learning opportunity. Offer stretch and development opportunities to team members, demonstrating you trust them and are invested in them learning and growing.

Step 2. Reflect on your intentional communication skills

As you reflect on the tools and techniques covered in this chapter to generate intentional communication, consider the following:

- As the leader of your team, are you taking an active part in the communication?

- Are you being intentional about *how* you speak up? Consider this in other teams you're a part of.

Advocacy vs Inquiry
Do you feel confident you can move between *advocacy and inquiry* with ease?

- Are there particular settings or people that you tend to use one over the other with?

- Which, generally, feels more comfortable for you: to ask questions and try to understand others' perspectives or to put forward an idea and move towards an outcome?

- What would it take for you to use your least preferred approach at times?

- How could you bring more balance to your conversations?

Consider a recent situation in which you found yourself wanting to challenge but were unclear about the best approach or, conversely, in a situation where you realised you advocated too strongly without hearing the perspective of others.

- Would the conversation have moved to a more productive outcome if you were able to balance between advocacy and inquiry?

- If you were to use the elements of the SAIL framework, how would you approach this conversation now?

As you review your responses to the above questions, what do you notice? Capture your reflections. Use the Team Presence Action Plan at the end of this chapter as a guide.

SAIL Framework
Consider a recent occasion where you have been in disagreement with a co-worker.

- As you reflect on your input into the conversation, break it down into the four elements of SAIL.

- Ask yourself: how well did I demonstrate each component?

- Now reflect on the input of others and reflect on the same question.

- What could you do differently next time?

As you review your responses to the above questions, what do you notice? Capture your reflections and add them to your Team Presence Action Plan.

Four Player Model
Review the Four Player Model and reflect on the following questions while considering a team you're a member of: (adapted from *Reading the Room* by David Kantor):

- How regularly do you initiate an action or suggest an option? (*move*)

- How regularly do you follow someone else's suggestion? (*follow*)

- How regularly do you oppose or challenge someone else's suggestion? (*oppose*)

- How regularly do you offer feedback and reflection on your observations of others' input? (*bystand*)

CHAPTER 6: TEAM PRESENCE

If you had to give a percentage equalling 100% for each of the above, how do you split your time across each of those speech acts – *move, follow, oppose, bystand* – when with your team? Do you tend to overuse or underuse any of the speech acts? If so, what is the impact? Do you see any 'stuck patterns' play out? Effective communication is about enabling all of the four speech acts as needed.

Do you recognise overuse or underuse in others? If so, how would you invite this speech act from them?

As you review the above questions and reflect on your use of the Four Player Model, what do you notice? Capture your reflections and add these to your Team Presence Action Plan.

Step 3. Create an action plan and develop your skills

Reflect on your responses in the above exercises and consider the steps you will take to refine your Team Presence. Use the following Team Presence Action plan to guide you.

TEAM PRESENCE ACTION PLAN: BRINGING IT ALL TOGETHER

Incorporate all that you have learnt in the previous chapters
- Keep in mind connecting to self is an ongoing self-reflective habit. Continue to practice this.
- Review your action plans from Chapters 4 and 5 for Inner Presence and Leadership Presence.

Practice intentional communication
- Advocacy vs inquiry
- SAIL framework
- The Four Player Model

Identify key focus areas to address, e.g I could bring more balance to conversations by:

_____

_____

_____

Develop your Team Presence
What does success look like? Key action steps

_____

_____

OVER TO YOU

At the beginning of this book I gave you a vision. I asked you to imagine yourself:
- working with a connected and collaborative team where you don't have to come up with all the answers
- not feeling like you have to keep pedalling faster and harder to succeed
- starting each day with energy and confidence.

I don't expect you to have attained that vision by the end of the book, but I have laid out a path to help you get there.

And you're already on the way.

You started with connecting to self – building a reflective habit and honing your self-regulation skills – which is the foundation work for each of the domains of presence.

You dug deep to look at your vision for the future and what really matters to you, and learnt how to draw upon this to remain calm and confident when the going gets tough (Inner Presence).

You've looked at the type of leader you want to be and explored how to get there through adopting leadership behaviours that build trust and connection (Leadership Presence).

And finally, you've learnt how bringing this together can cultivate an environment in which you and others can have respectful, open and robust conversations that generate productive outcomes while learning and innovating together (Team Presence).

You've got a complete 'presence toolkit' and an action plan.

Now, imagine that I waved a magic wand and you could implement everything on your action plan tomorrow. How would life look for you? You would come into work radiating energy and enthusiasm. You would feel grounded and confident as you navigated complexity and ambiguity. Your team would be motivated and engaged and feel interpersonally safe to take risks and be accountable for results: a high performing team. And they would be working collaboratively across teams.

Imagine if every company was like that. There would be no place for organisations full of tension and toxic interactions. Imagine that world.

What's the difference, really, between you and this goal? It's whether or not you take action. I want you to thrive in our complex and fast-paced world, so here's my recommendation: set aside some time every day or every week, work with a mentor, a coach or a peer and do the work. You will get results. I know because I've seen it happen again and again.

I wish you well.

RELATED READING

Throughout this book, I've mentioned many articles, journals, books and URLs where I've been inspired and informed by others. I've included the titles below as a further reading list and I hope these experts in their field will enlighten you as they have me.

Books

Amy Edmondson (2019) *The Fearless Organization*

Brené Brown (2018) *Dare To Lead*

Chris Argyris & Donald A. Schön (1996) *Organizational learning II: Theory, method and practice*

Daniel Pink (2006) *A Whole New Mind*

Daniel Goleman (1998) *Working with Emotional Intelligence*

David Kantor (2012) *Reading the Room*

Frederic Laloux (2016) *Reinventing Organizations*

Jim Clifton & Jim Harter (2019) *It's the Manager*

Joshua Freedman (2012) *At the Heart of Leadership*

Joshua Freedman & Massimiliano Ghini (2010) *Inside Change*

Kim Scott (2017) *Radical Candor*

Lynda Gratton (2011) *The Shift*

Malcolm Gladwell (2008) *Outliers*

Martin Seligman, (2011) *Flourish*

Simon Sinek (2013) *Start with Why*

Sylvia Ann Hewlett (2014) *Executive Presence*

William Isaacs (1999) *Dialogue: The Art of Thinking Together*

Articles and journals

Amy Cuddy, Matthew Kohut & John Neffinger (August 2013) 'Connect then Lead' *Harvard Business Review*

Christopher S Reina et al (May 2017) 'Quitting the Boss? The Role of Manager Influence

Tactics and Employee Emotional Engagement in
Voluntary Turnover'
Journal of Leadership and Organizational Studies

Daniel Ames & Francis Flynn (Jan 2007)
'What Breaks a Leader: The Curvilinear Relation
between Assertiveness and Leadership'
Journal of Personality and Social Psychology

Ernst & Young (2013)
'The Power of Many'
EYGM Limited

Fabio Sala (Sept 2003)
'Executive Blind Spots: Discrepancies Between Self-
and Other- Ratings'
Consulting Psychology Journal Practice and Research

Nihar Chhaya (July 2019)
'Does Your Leadership Style Scare Your Employees?'
Harvard Business Review

Peter Salovey & John Mayer (March 1990)
'Emotional Intelligence'
Imagination, Cognition and Personality Journal

Tasha Eurich (Jan 2018)
'What Self-Awareness Really Is (and How to Cultivate It)' *Harvard Business Review*

URLs

Charles Duhigg (February 2016)
'What Google Learned from its Quest to Build the Perfect Team'
nytimes.com/2016/02/28/magazine/what-google-learned-from-its-quest-to-build-the-perfect-team.html
The New York Times Magazine

Dan Cable (2019)
'Alive at Work'
store.hbr.org/product/alive-at-work-the-neuroscience-of-helping-your-people-love-what-they-do/10184

Tim Westergren (August 2013)
'Humble Mindset'
hbr.org/video/2363593483001/leadership-takes-humility
Harvard Business Review

WAYS TO KEEP IN TOUCH AND WORK TOGETHER

If you would like to talk about how you can build psychological safety, connection and engagement – to generate effective outcomes - within your team(s) or more broadly across your organisation, please get in touch.

Like any good project, input from others provides opportunities to discuss, reflect and refine. I welcome your feedback, observations and reflections about this book.

sheila.wherry@eiexecutive.com.au
www.eiexecutive.com.au.
or reach out via LinkedIn.

AUTHOR BIO

Sheila Wherry is an executive coach and consultant based in Sydney, Australia. Her career has spanned 30 years across international sales-management, coaching and consulting in Asia-Pacific, US and Europe.

She is a PCC credentialed coach of the International Coaching Federation and holds accreditations in various psychometric, evidence-based tools. With a masters in management and postgraduate qualifications in psychotherapy and executive coaching, she has taught a wide range of university classes, including strategic leadership (MBA level), organisational behaviour and conflict management.

Sheila works with leaders from a wide range of industry sectors and government departments, as well as owners of small to medium enterprises. Working with such a diverse range of people has cemented her belief that no matter what level of leadership or role you hold, the fundamental aspect of success and happiness is human connection. This is the foundation of her work.

GRATITUDE

This book was a collective endeavour and I am deeply grateful to those who have supported various stages of this creative process.

Let me start with Claudia Lantos. Thank you for throwing down the gauntlet and suggesting I write this book. You inspired me to take on something bigger than I'd imagined for myself.

To Leanne Mills and Crissa Sumner. Thank you for reading the entire first manuscript and sharing invaluable feedback and suggestions to take this book project to the next level. I am so appreciative of this and for your friendship. Thank you also to clients, colleagues, family and friends who have read sections, given feedback and encouraged me onwards.

To my book coach, Kath Walters, who so artfully found the balance between holding me to account to meet our tight deadlines, while offering tremendous support and encouragement to get me through the writing process and to a first draft. I wouldn't have got here without you.

To my immensely talented editor, Lu Sexton, for your input, support and guidance which has helped appreciably shape this book. Thank you for partnering with me on this journey. Your humour has kept me sane in the final stages of this project.

To my clients, thank you for trusting me enough to be willing to drop your masks, look within and take yourself on. This takes courage and I never take this lightly. It is a privilege to work with you and it is a joy to see your results. While you may recognise your situation in the client stories in this book, I can assure you these are drawn from a composite of common themes gathered from multiple clients over many years.

To my parents, who just love me at every turn. No matter what I do, you rally from the sidelines, while continuing to remind me that nothing is more important than the people I love. Thank you, Mum, for listening to me talk on and on about this book while we spent many mornings walking around Centennial Park. I'm so grateful for the time we share. And to Cliff, for offering your stories and for being an inspiration to me. Your kind-hearted soul and accepting nature is something to behold. How lucky I am to call you Dad.

And finally, to Kylie and Connor, my partner and son, who have been extraordinarily patient as I've disappeared for days upon days to write. And at other times when I have been physically there but not *present* (instead, writing in my head). The irony is not lost on me. How incredibly lucky I am to call you both 'home'.

www.ingramcontent.com/pod-product-compliance
Lightning Source LLC
Chambersburg PA
CBHW070256010526
44107CB00056B/2475